EMBROIDERY
from a
COUNTRY BARN

EMBROIDERY
from a
COUNTRY BARN

GAIL BETT • DEBORAH McNAB • LOU STINSON

A RATHDOWNE BOOK

ALLEN & UNWIN

© Gail Bett, Deborah McNab and Louise Stinson 1994

Photographs by Neil Lorimer
Styling by Penny Smith
Designed by text-art

First published in 1994

A Rathdowne Book
Allen & Unwin Pty Ltd
9 Atchison Street
St Leonards NSW 2065, Australia

10 9 8 7 6 5 4 3 2 1

National Library of Australia
cataloguing-in-publication data

Bett, Gail.
    Embroidery from a country barn.

    Bibliography.
    ISBN 1 86373 619 0.

    1. Needlework. 2. Handicraft. I. McNab, Deborah. II. Stinson, Louise. III. Lorimer, Neil. IV. Title.

746.44

Printed by South Wind Production, Singapore

Photograph opposite title page: The appliquéd sun centre on the Sunshine Quilt (instructions on page 40)

CONTENTS

ACKNOWLEDGEMENTS

We thank Millicent Gould for sewing the Gumnut Footstool, Heather Scott for sewing the Poppy Rose Footstool, Ann Herbert for providing us with pre-loved Oxford cloth school shirts and Heather Guthrie, Rosie Webb, Sue Cass, Honey Murphy, Anne Fleming, Marg Cook and Joyce Whitbourne for various tasks they did so willingly.

Also we thank those who have helped us with sound advice at some of our suppliers, especially our friends at Les Olivades and Bargello.

Thank you to Decollo of Armadale and Wardlow of Hawthorn, Melbourne, for providing fabrics for use in some of the photographs.

Thank you Julie Gibbs for your initial suggestion for this book and for your enthusiasm in steering our course through very uncharted waters.

And of course to Bob, Duncan and Bobby and our offspring for not doubting and for being patient.

INTRODUCTION

The impetus for this book arose out of common interest, shared goals and close friendship. All three of us live on properties in Victoria in the hills surrounding Geelong and a focus for us all is the barn on the Bett property where we meet regularly to stitch and dream up new projects, and to laugh a lot.

This book combines various talents individual to each of us. Debo is our designer, our artist. Debo likes to see possibilities in all aspects of life as springboards for art. She dips into literature, art, nature, craft and even into rubbish tips. Her perceptive eye and ability to translate immediate impressions into lasting pictures is clearly in evidence in this book. Debo is an infectiously enthusiastic person and is never afraid to experiment with various materials. When not actually doing farm work, you may find Debo busy dyeing, sketching, knitting or painting. She has a firm belief in the universality of strong ancient design and the use of colour combinations throughout the centuries. Debo is constantly showing us examples from the past of designs and colour combinations suggested as 'modern'.

Gail also has a strong flair for colour and design. She has been responsible for all the beautiful stitching and for reining in Debo's design fantasies, so they become accessible to sewers of various capabilities. She shows her keen interest in the mix of texture and colour by using many different stitches and threads. Gail has a sharp eye for detail and a much envied ability in and love of rearrangement. It is not surprising to find a room of the Bett farmhouse completely different to the way it was the month before. These comments may make Gail sound rather daunting, but this is not true; her ability to easily convey ideas and dispel fears and to coax the best out of individuals are attributes her many students will attest to. Gail is not a 'follow the rule' person and thinks of these projects merely as beginnings.

My job is to put into words the creativity and skills of my two partners in such a way as to capture their abundant enthusiasm and spirit and at the same time to provide clear instructions for sewers. Sometimes I have completed the projects myself to test the clarity of my written instructions. With my teaching background, I share with Gail and Debo a keen regard for the sharing of knowledge and imparting of skills. I believe a teacher's role is to open doors—as a teacher of literature I always hoped my ex-students would be able to read through new eyes.

All three of us hope the readers and users of this book will be keener observers and will see stitching possibilities in both obscure and very ordinary places.

HELPFUL HINTS

BEGINNING AND FINISHING OFF WORK

Unlike traditional embroiderers Gail likes to use a knot for every sewing thread. To finish off she does two little stitches, takes her needle through the second stitch, and runs a little bit of the thread through the stitching for a strong finish.

MAKING A LIGHT BOX FROM A FRUIT BOX

We have found a light box invaluable for tracing designs onto cloth, even as thick as crewel linen. If the fabric is thick, you may have to go over the design with a thick felt tip pen so you can see it clearly through the fabric. We like to trace the design using a very sharp 6B lead pencil.

An easy way to make a light box is with a polystyrene foam fruit box. Cut a hole on a bottom edge big enough to put the plug of an electrical cord through. A small bedside lamp with a strong globe is inserted in the bottom and a piece of glass is then placed across the top. Put several rows of masking or electrician's tape around the edge of the glass so it is not sharp.

Remember not to leave your light globe on too long otherwise the polystyrene might melt.

NEEDLES

You will need a selection of needles. The head of the needle should always be the thickness of your threads—you don't want to have a bigger eye in the needle than the threads you are using and vice versa. The needles used in this book are:

Number 7 Embroidery Crewel needles for Stranded cottons
    and Silks
Calico Braided Rug needles for heavy work
Chenille needles for wools and Perle cottons and Watercolours threads
Appliqué needles for fine sewing and piecing
Quilting needles
Tapestry needles

THREADS

When using wools it is important to find the right and wrong way to thread the needle. Run your fingers along the thread in each direction to find the smooth and the rough nap of the thread. Thread your needle with the top end of the smooth nap. This means you are sewing with the twist of the thread and it will not wear thin as quickly. When using two threads of wool, they must always be threaded this same way; do not use a long strand of wool and fold it over.

To make quilting threads last longer and to prevent them from twisting and knotting while you sew, thread your needle from the spool before you cut it. The length of all your threads should measure from your thumb to your elbow.

EMBROIDERY FRAMES

Gail believes the best results are achieved by using an embroidery ring or hoop. The hoop keeps the work taut, centred on the straight of the grain, and stops it puckering, especially when Satin stitching. The hoop also helps keep your stitches uniform. Binding the inner ring with cotton tape protects the work and holds it better. Always be sure to remove your work from the frame between work sessions.

HOW TO WASH YOUR WORK

It is often not necessary to wash your work. If you do, the best way is to dip it into a bucket of lukewarm water with soft washing detergent, mild dishwashing liquid and a dessert-spoon of salt. Wash gently until you are happy it is clean, gently squeeze the water from it and rinse in clean lukewarm water. Do not allow it to soak in water. Roll it up in a towel and give it a good pummel to help the towel absorb the water. Iron while damp on a towel, using a warm iron and pressing the work on the wrong side. While ironing you can ease the work to its proper shape. Leave until bone dry and give the work another press.

THE PHOTOCOPIER

Debo finds this is a marvellous companion to design. You should keep an 'inspiration' file with bits photocopied from not only the print medium, but plants, dead insects, bits of china, feathers, fabric, lace, etc. Any of these bits may be a springboard to design. Don't forget to record the name and date of publication of your printed reference, as you may wish to return to the source years later. You can use magic tape to stick bits on to make a collage of several different elements.

You should copy every stage of a developing drawing so if your experiments go wrong, you can revert to the original. You can trace a design, then copy it in reverse to make a repeat. Enlarge or reduce the sizes dramatically to give different design perspectives. You can also make two identical copies of your line drawing—on one, colour the design shapes in a dark colour, and on the other, colour in the background, for an entirely different effect.

Try photocopying our Ex Libris and working a design for a border from this source or any other motif in the book.

COLOUR

This is absolutely personal! Debo mostly loves bright, energetic colours, but she is also passionate about pastels and sometimes is surprised to find black and white the only choice. Buy a colour wheel to find out which colours go together and what fun you can have with colour dissonance!

Gail thinks it is important to keep in mind the need to balance concentrations of colour across your work. In looking at the workpiece overall it is helpful to think triangularly. If a strong colour is placed at the peak of the triangle, then it is usually as well to have this colour at the two base corners. Arranging your dominant colours around the points of an imagined triangle will help you achieve a successful colour balance.

Debo likes to use a lot of dark or black outlines to firmly establish the basic shape which you can treat with various stitches, shades or threads. High contrast lends drama and vivacity, just like matt surfaces make shining ones sparkle.

Overall Debo's chief advice is not to be afraid to experiment. Always go a little over the top, as it is much easier to salvage a glorious extravagance than it is to inspire a stodgy start.

OTHER ALLIES TO DESIGN

When constructing a design, exaggerate the shapes and curves. Don't draw them unenthusiastically or your finished work will lack animation. The drawing should have the feeling of only just containing the energy of the fruit, flowers, animals or whatever else you are joyously creating.

Several thicknesses of nibs in drawing pens are helpful. Debo prefers a waterproof line so you can wash in colours after you have basic shapes established. Watercolour paints or thicker gouache should become your friends. Graph paper, tracing paper, white-out pen used like a paint brush, and a magnifying glass are all allies in Debo's design work.

HOW TO APPROACH THIS BOOK

Many of the designs in this book appear slightly complicated and wordy in their explanation but don't be daunted, they are much easier in their execution. Seek some of the easier projects to start off with: the Curtain Keepers, Rosie's Braided Cushion or the Garlanded Antimacassar. The Gumnut Footstool has only four different stitches, while the Lurking Fox Seat Cover has only two. Step-by-step instructions for sewing each stitch are provided in the Stitch Glossary at the back of the book. Stitches contained in the Glossary are capitalised in the text.

This book is not intended as a textbook, but should be a springboard to further individual ideas of design and stitching. We have found if you leave room for happy accidents they often oblige by turning up.

CHAPTER ❦ ONE

KILIMS AND BEYOND

Kilims are flat, woven rugs distinct from knotted, pile rugs. Perfection was said to have been attained by the Kashan weavers of central Persia in the seventeenth century. Fineness of detail characterised these rugs. Designs resembled fine miniatures crowded with figures and animal forms, often in floral settings. This all sounds bucolic and decorative until you examine in detail the menacing looks and the lurking gait of some of the animals; a distinct air of threat is nearly always apparent.

Our kilim creatures were painted freehand whilst gazing into an ancient kilim with a large magnifying glass. It becomes apparent these rugs were born of a hunting people. The animals and birds that are depicted are either hunting or being hunted. The fox casts a cunning glance over his shoulder as he closes in on his prey. The rabbit leaps from the fox, while the goose high-steps in retreat. The deer also is in flight with mouth open, tongue out maybe in fear. If this scenario is true the pheasants are vulnerable! It is the leaping quality which struck Debo's fancy and Gail has captured their movement in colourful stitches. In all these animals and birds the traditional shapes are preserved from the seventeenth century, however, instead of becoming dead and flat, we hope the richly contrasting colours and movements help to animate today's embroidery.

Although these animals have been stitched on seat covers, a tea-cosy, a hot-water bottle cover, a stool and a satchel, they would be very stylish as a set of six chair seats.

THE LURKING FOX SEAT COVER

This wary fox is colourfully stitched on a small piece of Homespun (cotton material) before being appliquéd onto your chosen seat cover fabric (see photograph on page 4). A fairly dark fabric is the best to choose.

MATERIALS REQUIRED:

Indian cotton or cushion fabric—50 cm (20 in)
Homespun—25 cm (10 in)
Piecemaker Calico Braided Rug needle
Piecemaker Chenille needle
Appletons wools—charcoal grey 926 and lemon 841
Select a combination of DMC Perle 5 and DMC Stranded
    cotton in these colours—white, black, red 321, blue
    796, gold 729, 422, yellow 307, green 319, 911, maroon
    3685 and mauve 327

Enlarge the fox illustration on a photocopier by 122%. Trace the outline of the fox onto the Homespun.

The flowers are worked first. The petals are Short and Long stitch using a combination of DMC Perle 5 and DMC Stranded cotton. They are outlined in Split Back stitch. The centre of the flowers are Satin stitch. Choose colours thoughtfully.

The background is filled with Split Back stitch using one thread of charcoal grey Appletons wool.

The eye is worked in six threads of white DMC Stranded cotton using Stem stitch and is outlined in black DMC Stranded Split Back stitch.

The tummy is worked in lemon Appletons wool in Split Back stitch. The body and legs are then outlined in six strands of black DMC Stranded cotton using Split Back stitch.

Appliqué the fox onto your chosen fabric then Split Back stitch around the outside of the fox using red DMC Stranded cotton. Sew an outer row in Stem stitch in red DMC Perle 5.

The seat cover is then made up according to the size of your chair.

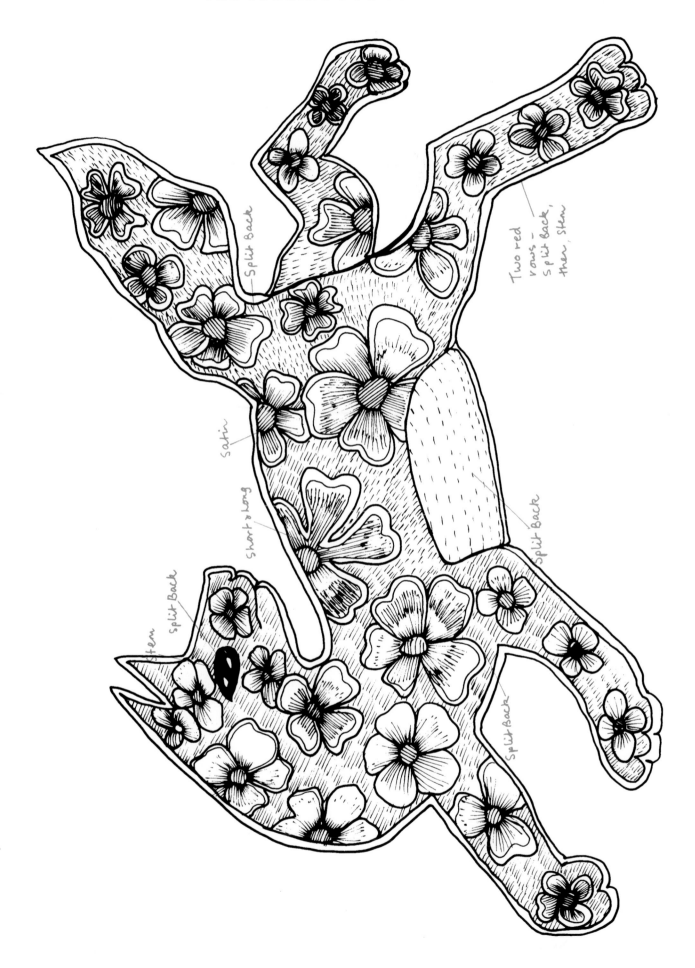

THE LEAPING HARE SEAT COVER

MATERIALS REQUIRED:

Homespun—25 cm (10 in)
Indian cotton or cushion fabric—50 cm (20 in)
Piecemaker Calico Braided Rug needle
Piecemaker Chenille needle
Appletons wool—plum 102, charcoal grey 926, red 501 and
    sky blue 463
Watercolours thread—Flame
Rachael 100 per cent nylon thread—gold
DMC Perle 5 and DMC Stranded cottons—white, black, red
    321, blue 796, orange 946, 422, yellow 444, green 319,
    911, maroon 3685 and mauve 327

Enlarge the hare illustration overleaf on a photocopier by
122%. The hare is then traced onto the Homespun.

The yellow spots are worked first in Satin stitch using DMC
Perle 5. The red and blue centres are worked in the same
thread and stitch. At the very centre of the yellow spots stitch
a small Back stitch in green.

The centre of the plum background is worked in Split Back
stitch with one thread of Appletons wool, working the stitches
up and down vertically. This centre section is then outlined
in green Stem stitch using three threads of DMC Stranded
cotton. The 'rib cage' is worked in Cretan stitch using
Watercolours Flame. The outline of this ribbing is worked in
three threads of DMC Stranded cotton using Stem stitch. This
'rib cage' stitching continues down the four legs.

The orange and red spots on the head and tail are all worked
in Satin stitch using DMC Perle 5. The orange spots on the
body are in Satin stitch too. The inside of the ear is Short and
Long stitch using red DMC Perle 5 and gold Rachael. The
tummy patch is Split Back stitch in Appletons wool, with red
and gold on the underside in either wool or Stranded cotton.
The eye is worked in white Satin stitch and outlined in black
Stem stitch.

The body, head and ears are worked in Split Back stitch using
one thread of charcoal grey Appletons wool. The legs and tail
are worked the same way in sky blue Appletons wool and
outlined in six strands of black DMC Stranded cotton using
Split Back stitch.

*The Lurking Fox
Seat Cover
(instructions on
page 2)*

The hare is then appliquéd onto your chosen fabric and
outlined in two rows—one of Split Back stitch using six
strands of red DMC Stranded cotton, and the other Stem stitch
in red DMC Perle 5. The seat cover can now be made up.

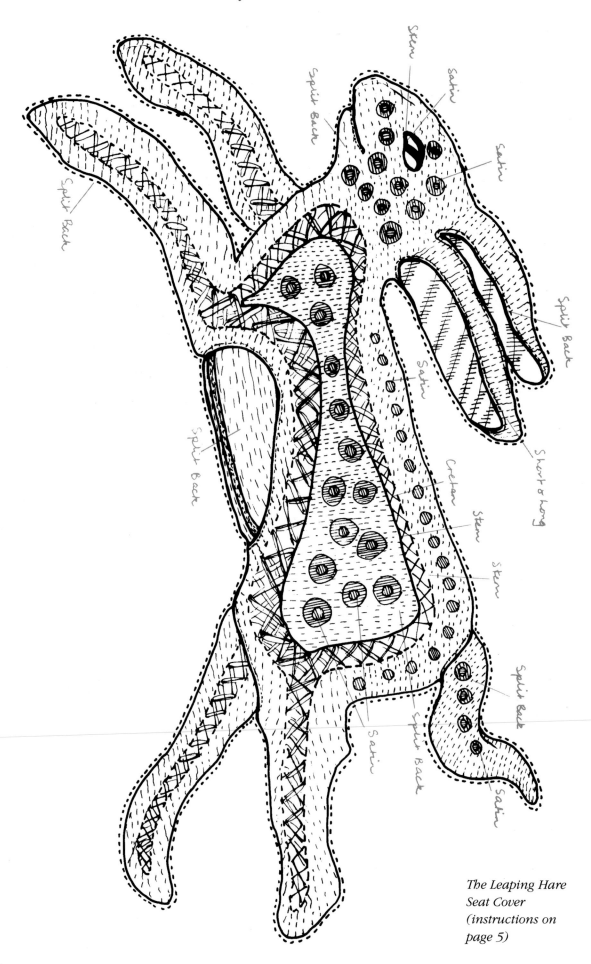

The Leaping Hare
Seat Cover
(instructions on
page 5)

FRUIT TREE PHEASANTS STOOL

This is an exciting project ideally suited to variegated threads as well as stranded threads. The variegated threads, from a company called Watercolours in Connecticut, USA, are hand-dyed. The company was started by Lois Caron after she became frustrated by the lack of imaginative colours in threads. From dyeing for herself in kitchen pots she has moved to an export industry. The threads arrive in three strands and we use just one strand in sewing here. The gradation of colour changes imperceptibly as you sew. When you start on the lighter end of one thread and sew to the dark end, begin your next thread with the dark end to blend the colours naturally. This thread is excellent for birds, fruit, flowers—anything living which benefits from a touch of vivacity.

Debo's husband Duncan, a woodworker of distinction, made the stool for these pheasants from a piece of oak wood blown down on a property in the Moorabool valley.

MATERIALS REQUIRED:

Strong, Indian-type cotton—1 m (3 ft)
Watercolours threads—Ice, Tobacco, Bark, Blueberry,
    Flame and Peacock
DMC Stranded cotton—722, 3051, 3052, 347, 792, 817 and
    920
DMC Perle 5—726, 535 and 743

Enlarge the illustration on a photocopier by 141%. Trace the illustration onto a strong Indian-type cotton using a 5B pencil and a light box.

The main trunk of the tree is sewn first in Split Back stitch in Watercolours Tobacco thread. The thinner branches are worked in three rows of Split Back stitch, while the thicker branches are sewn in additional rows to construct the thickness. These branches are also sewn using Watercolours Tobacco thread.

The fruit are worked next in yellow DMC Perle 5—726 in Roumanian Couching, which gives the correct texture. Where there is some shading in the fruit, overstitch in Roumanian Couching using two threads of DMC Stranded cotton—920.

Next the leaves are worked in Fly stitch using four strands of DMC Stranded cotton—3051 and 3052 for darker and lighter tones. The leaves and fruit are joined to the branches with a thread of Watercolours Blueberry or Watercolours Tobacco using Split Back stitch.

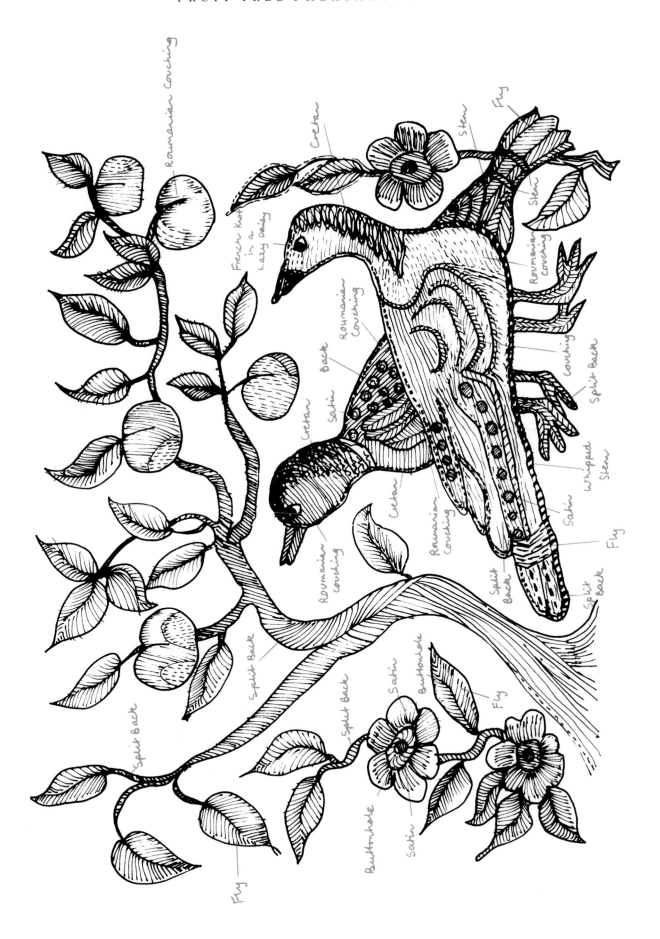

In sewing the pheasants, start with the cock bird in the rear. The hood of the head is Cretan stitch in Watercolours Flame. The rest of the head is worked in Roumanian Couching in two threads of DMC Stranded cotton—722. The wing of this bird is three rows of Cretan stitch using Watercolours Tobacco. The spots on the back are red Satin stitch spots in two threads of DMC Stranded cotton—347 and are outlined in small Back stitch using Watercolours Blueberry. Fill in the back with Roumanian Couching in Watercolours Ice. The breast is worked in Roumanian Couching using two threads of DMC Stranded cotton—722. The tail feathers of the cock bird are four rows of Fly stitch using DMC Stranded cotton—722. The bands of red colour are worked in Stem stitch using Watercolours Flame. The beak is Roumanian Couching using Watercolours Flame. The bird will come to life when you give it an eye—a French Knot encased in a Lazy Daisy stitch using Watercolours Blueberry.

The hen bird's hood is Cretan stitch in Watercolours Blueberry. The head is Roumanian Couching using two threads of DMC Stranded cotton—722. The feathers of the wing are sewn in Split Back stitch in Watercolours Ice, working spots in Satin stitch over the Split Back stitch in four threads of DMC Stranded cotton—792. The outline of the wing is Split Back stitch in DMC Stranded cotton—792. The lines on the wings are four threads of the same cotton Couched down. The rest of the body and the other tail feathers are two strands of DMC Stranded cotton—722, sewn in Roumanian Couching. The tail tip of the bottom two feathers is worked across with six rows of Fly stitch using Watercolours Flame. A stitch of blue is sewn in between each red stitch. Three little blue stitches run along the centre of each tail tip. The beak and eye are the same as for the cock bird. The feet of both birds are worked in Split Back stitch using Watercolours Flame.

Both the birds are outlined in Stem stitch using one thread of Watercolours Flame. The Stem stitch of the hen bird's underside is whipped in DMC Stranded cotton—792.

The very centre of the blossoms are worked horizontally in four threads of DMC Stranded cotton—792. Surrounding the blue, sew Satin stitch vertically in one thread of Watercolours Flame. The petals are worked in Satin stitch using Watercolours Tobacco. When you complete this, a row of Buttonhole stitch is worked around the centre and into the petals, using two threads of DMC Stranded cotton—817.

Opposite: Fruit Tree Pheasants Stool (instructions start on page 8)

The leaves are worked in the same way as the leaves on the tree and in the same colours but outline them in Buttonhole stitch using two threads of DMC Stranded cotton—817. The leaves are joined to the flowers with Split Back stitch using Watercolours Bark.

The picture is now ready for its border. Draw faint lines in a rectangle around the embroidered image: the inner border measures 30 cm x 26.5 cm (12 in x 10¾ in), the outer border measures 34.5 cm x 31 cm (14 in x 12½ in). Sew the inside row first, which is two rows of Chain stitch using Watercolours Flame. Then stitch a row of Stem stitch using DMC Perle 5—535. The next row is Cretan stitch using DMC Perle 5—743, with uneven spots of red and blue—Watercolours Flame and Ice—in amongst the Cretan stitch. Another row of Stem stitch in DMC Perle 5—535 is sewn. This row is followed by two rows of Chain stitch using Watercolours Flame and a row of Chain stitch using Watercolours Peacock. Finally, stitch a row of Chain stitch using Watercolours Blueberry.

In the corner triangles, the outside line is Chain stitch using Watercolours Ice laced with Watercolours Blueberry. Inside the triangle two rows of Chain stitch using Watercolours Blueberry are stitched and finally one row of Chain stitch using DMC Stranded cotton—817. A French Knot in the same thread is sewn in the centre of this last triangle.

THE DEAR DEER HOT-WATER BOTTLE COVER

The deer was our 'Oh dear, a pale deer'. We all thought one of our kilim group should be sewn in pale colours to see the possibilities of tasteful pastels. Inevitably with us he kept growing a little stronger and cheekier, and now he has a life of his own. We have him on a soft cotton hot-water bottle cover with a woollen padding insert (see photograph on page 15), but he can be enlarged and can join the other kilim group as a seat cover. He would look just right on a box lid, too.

The deer is worked on a piece of plain coloured Homespun which is then appliquéd onto soft cotton. He can also be sewn directly onto soft cotton.

MATERIALS REQUIRED:

Homespun—25 cm (10 in)
Soft cotton material—40 cm (16 in)
Blanket offcut—30 cm (12 in) square
Watercolours threads—Tobacco, Rose Blush and Ice
DMC Perle 5—932, 844
DMC Stranded cotton—white, 844, 317 and 221

Enlarge the illustration overleaf on a photocopier by 141% then trace onto the Homespun. The whole of the body is sewn in Roumanian Couching running the length of the body and across the legs as shown in the drawing. Watercolours Tobacco is the thread used. For the chest, the pinkier tones of the thread are used to give a shaded effect. The legs are sewn in Watercolours Rose Blush.

One half of each circle on the deer's body is stitched in DMC Perle 5—932 in tight Buttonhole stitch. The rest of the circle is filled in with white Satin stitch using six strands of DMC Stranded cotton in a spot on the circle—see the drawing. The circles are then edged in Stem stitch using DMC Perle 5—844.

On the underneath of the tail sew Buttonhole stitch in DMC Perle 5—844. The body and tail have spots of French Knots worked in two threads of DMC Stranded cotton—some in 844, some in 317, and the rest in 221. On the legs French Knots are sewn in DMC Stranded cotton—221.

The different parts of the body are outlined in Stem stitch in DMC Perle 5—844. The hooves are Satin stitch in the same thread. The ears are Satin stitch in the pink tones of Watercolours Tobacco. The undersides of the ears are outlined in the same colour using Roumanian Couching, while the tongue is

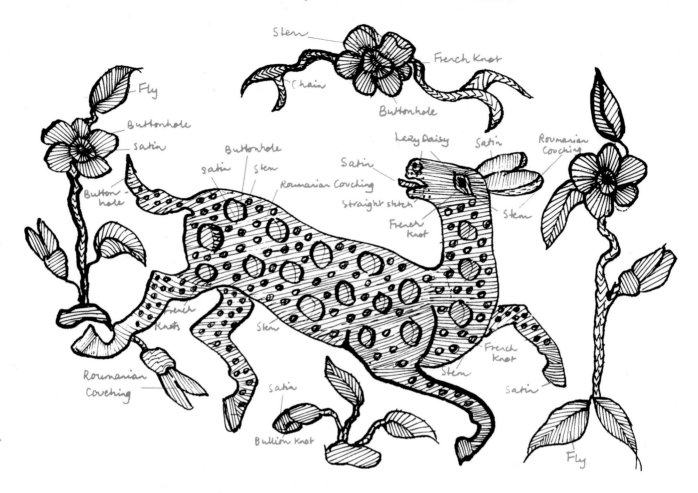

Satin stitch in the same colour. The nostril is a black Lazy Daisy stitch in DMC Perle 5—844. A white Lazy Daisy stitch lies next to it. The spots around the mouth are a little straight stitch, in one thread of 844. The eye is white Satin stitch with a Lazy Daisy stitch in the middle in 844. In the very centre is a French Knot. The eye is outlined in 844 with Stem stitch.

The deer is now ready to be appliquéd onto the soft cotton. The flowers and leaves are worked directly onto the fabric. The top flower has a French Knot in the centre in white DMC Stranded cotton, and the side pink flowers have Satin stitch in the middle. The petals are worked in Buttonhole stitch: the side flowers in the same tones of Watercolours Tobacco which are used in sewing the deer, the top flower in Watercolours Ice. A pink circle of Buttonhole stitch is worked out from the centre of each flower. The buds on the side branches are Roumanian Couching.

Most of the leaves are Fly stitch using Watercolours Ice. The leaves beneath the deer are in Fly stitch and Satin stitch in the greeny tones of Watercolours Tobacco. The bud of this group of leaves is sewn in Satin stitch in Watercolours Ice with a pink Bullion Knot. The stems are all worked in Chain stitch in Watercolours Tobacco.

The final task is to Stem stitch around the appliquéd deer in DMC Perle 5—844. The hot-water bottle cover can be made to a number of patterns.

The Dear Deer Hot-Water Bottle Cover (instructions start on page 13)

THE STRUTTING GOOSE
TEA-COSY

We have worked this high-stepping goose onto a tea-cosy (see photograph on page 18). He would be equally good on the pocket of a cotton or viyella shirt or a child's pyjamas. The goose is another traditional kilim bird, so he could become part of the chair cover set with the hare and fox. Our goose was worked on Homespun and then appliquéd onto a thick fabric, one which would keep the teapot warm without being padded.

MATERIALS REQUIRED:

Homespun—20 cm (8 in)
Tea-cosy fabric—quite sturdy—25 cm (10 in)
Piecemaker Calico Braided Rug needle
Piecemaker Chenille needle
DMC Perle 5—946, 817 and Ecru
DMC Stranded cotton—413, 317 and 3753

Reduce illustration on a photocopier by 82% and trace the outline onto the Homespun.

Work the tail feathers first in orange continuous Fly stitches close together using DMC Perle 5—946. Over these open Fly stitch is stitched with two strands of DMC Stranded cotton—413. Next work the fluffy back feathers in Buttonhole using two strands of alternating colours of grey, DMC Stranded cotton 413 and 317. The base of the wing is Roumanian Couching using two strands of DMC Stranded cotton—3753. Stitch French Knots in grey DMC Stranded cotton—413 over the top to create the speckles.

Work the red claws in Roumanian Couching using DMC Perle 5—817. The beak is Satin stitch using the same red.

Gail stitched the body and legs using Tussah Silk from the Designer Silk Range. An alternative thread is DMC Perle 5—Ecru. The stitch here is Roumanian Couching following the flow of the lines on the drawing.

The eye is a French Knot encircled with a Lazy Daisy stitch using two strands of DMC Stranded cotton—413.

The goose is then appliquéd onto the tea-cosy fabric using slip stitches which are as invisible as possible. Work around the outside of the goose with Stem stitch in DMC Stranded—413. As well as the outline, highlight certain features of the bird also

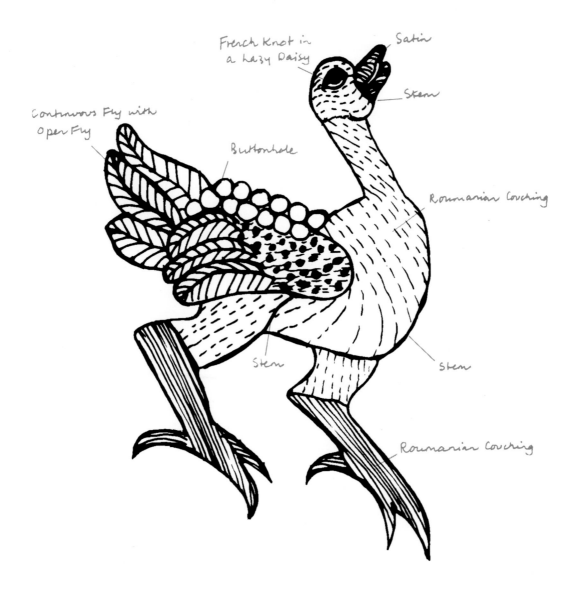

French Knot in
a Lazy Daisy

Satin

Stem

Continuous Fly with
Open Fly

Buttonhole

Roumanian Couching

Stem

Stem

Stem

Roumanian Couching

using Stem stitch in the same thread, for instance, separate the beak with these stitches.

Our tea-cosy is oval. You can make your tea-cosy any shape you like.

PAINTED PONY SATCHEL

The painted pony satchel might be a meeting stopper. We named him 'The Pony Express' for a while; he looked just like a courier. He is vivid and full of flair, just right for the busy executive to enter a meeting with panache! He would look different again on black fabric as a seat cover; the black would throw the colours into higher relief. You may want to tone him down if he is too bright for you—though his ears and hooves should always have a ritzy glitz to them!

MATERIALS REQUIRED:

Homespun—25 cm (10 in)
Indian Cotton—50 cm (20 in)
Piecemaker Calico Braided Rug needle
Piecemaker Chenille needle
Watercolours thread—Tobacco
Rachael 100 per cent nylon thread—gold
DMC Perle 5—844, 946, 602, 3347, 797, 444, 550, 817, 435, 469, 597, 931, 310, 725 and 223

Enlarge the illustration on a photocopier by 122%. Trace the pony outline onto the Homespun and work the embroidery on this before appliquéing it onto sturdy Indian cotton. All the stitches are alternating bands of Roumanian Couching and Split Back stitch. Each band is then separated with a row of Chain stitch using DMC Perle 5—844. The bands of stitching are worked in DMC Perle 5 with the occasional Watercolours thread. You can use your own colours; the ones we used are suggested here. Follow the photograph colours on page 22.

Starting at the tail and working across the body, the orange is 946, the crimson 602, the green 3347, the crimson 602, the blue 797, the green 3347, the yellow 444, the purple 550, yellow 444, the red 817, the brown 4435, the blue 797, the green 3347, different green 469, and the red 817.

The neck is 931 and Watercolours Tobacco with a row of Roumanian Couching in 931 sewn through the centre of the Tobacco band, then blue 797 and red 817. The nose is the pinkier tones of Watercolours Tobacco in Roumanian Couching. The mouth is Split Back stitch in 844 with a line of Roumanian Couching in orange 946. This is separated by a line of Chain stitch in 844. The rest of the head is worked in Roumanian Couching using 597. The eye is three rows of white Satin stitch outlined in dark grey 310 in Stem stitch, with a French Knot in the centre. The forelock is worked in two rows of Roumanian Couching outlined in Chain stitch in 844. The undersides of the ears are Roumanian Couching in

The Strutting Goose Tea-Cosy (instructions on page 16)

19

Watercolours Tobacco with little grey stitches worked at random to form spots. The top of the ears are bands of Roumanian Couching worked horizontally in Rachael, a 100 per cent gold nylon tubular thread which gives a shiny, wet look. Over the top of the gold, stitch two rows of three Chain stitches in 844. The ears are outlined in 844 in Chain stitch.

The rear hind leg is worked first in blue 797, then orange 946, then yellow 444 and banana 725. The stitching is Roumanian Couching sewn lengthways from the top of the leg to the bottom. These colours are separated by a row of Chain stitch in 844. The other hind leg is worked the same way in blue 797 and red 817. The hind hooves are a row of Split Back stitch in crimson 602, and two rows of Roumanian Couching in 931. The hooves are sewn in the gold Rachael thread in Satin stitch.

The very front leg is a band of Roumanian Couching in blue 797 and orange 946 parallelling down the leg and separated by Chain stitch in 844. The other front leg is a band of red 817 which continues from the body down and a band of yellow 444 separated by Chain stitch in 844.

Both front hooves are a row of Roumanian Couching in crimson 602 and then four rows or so of Roumanian Couching in 223. The hooves are again sewn in gold Rachael thread in Satin stitch.

Appliqué the pony onto the cotton using slip stitches which are as invisible as possible. Then work around the outside of the pony with Stem stitch in dark grey 310.

Faintly draw crossing lines 5 cm (2 in) apart across the Indian cotton and stitch with a tiny running or quilting stitch. This effect is called Cross-hatching.

We made up a satchel with the dimensions 30 cm x 43 cm (12 in x 17¼ in), an ideal size for holding a clipboard. The satchel has two zips on the back—a long and a short one.

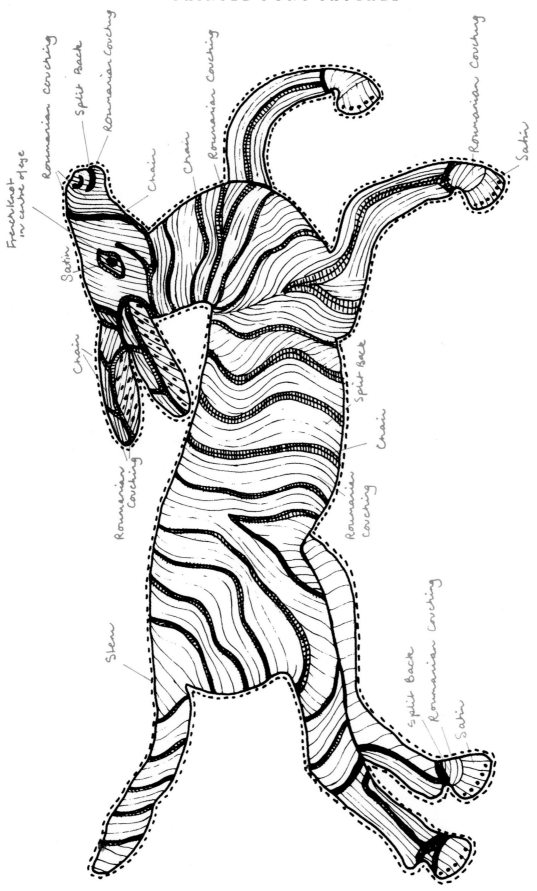

PROVENÇAL PROMPTED

Provence is a long way literally and metaphorically from Paris. After spending ten months living in Provence with my family, I inferred to a Parisian that my son spoke fluent French. She asked where we had been living. I replied, '23 kilometres from Marseille'. She laughed and replied, 'Well he certainly would not speak French'. To Parisians the Midi, or Provence, is very much of the earth, with less sophistication. Les Olivades materials capture this rustic quality. These cottons have a vibrant saturation of colour which is evocative of oranges, olives, lavender, broom and the blue of summer sea and sky. These fabrics are not the precious, pale brocades of a Parisian salon; they have a clarity all their own.

The fabrics have become fashionable in recent years, however their popularity dates back to the Renaissance when local French workshops produced imitations of successful Indian imports. In the seventeenth century the Kings of France had to forbid these French imitations as their popularity superseded original French designs. However, contraband production continued in the Papal territories of Provence—for example, in Avignon. A hundred years later this prohibition ended; it had actually increased the popularity of these materials. The ancestor of today's best known company, Souleiado, was founded near Tarascon following the French Revolution. In 1976 cousins of the same family branched out to establish Les Olivades, now the only producer which uses the same printing processes of earlier times: a flat frame rather than a rotating drum.

Something all three of us are interested in is the marrying of tradition and innovation...how century-old models can serve as inspirations for today's work. What characterises Les Olivades fabrics are particular patterns, the interpretation of certain themes such as the cachemire swirl, the Imperial bee from Napoleonic times, or the Pompadour bouquet. These

Painted Pony Satchel (instructions on page 19)

symbols translate well into modern fabrics. Debo and Gail have tried to pick up on these motifs of sun and flowers in designs for quilts, an antimacassar, tablemats, a cushion and tie-backs for curtains.

We have spent a lot of time in the Les Olivades shop in High Street, Armadale—a suburb in Melbourne—with its exciting selection of materials and particularly helpful staff. This shop has a direct link to the mill in France. Orders placed for fabric can be in Marseille very quickly and out here in a week. There are a few things to remember when using these cottons. They are pricey, but they are wide—1.5 m (5 ft)—and they come in two weights, both suitable for quilting. The decorative borders are printed in repeating bands and are sold by the metre. You will find seven or eight borders to 1 m (3 ft). These 'bandes' can be easily joined, making them ideal for edging your work.

The various patterns and colours of Les Olivades fabrics mix and match well as individual colours are repeated in individual designs. On the other hand, the patterns are usually busy and complex which enables them to complement simple, plain cottons. The simpler the design of your quilt the better with these materials—they shimmer and glow easily.

THE GARLANDED ANTIMACASSAR

The garland is a familiar design shape for embroiderers. This centrepiece garland combines appliqué overlaid with various embroidery stitches. Gail and Debo would like to acknowledge inspiration for this garland from D. Hinson's *American Graphic and Quilt Design*. We have used scraps of Les Olivades fabric, but any scraps would do in any arrangement. With this project you should use what we have given as a starting point for your imagination. As you work with this piece you will hopefully find yourself experimenting with both colours and stitches.

MATERIALS REQUIRED:

Homespun—61 cm (24 in) square—allow for seams
Cotton scraps
Border material—12 cm (5¾ in) wide—allow for seams
Batting—90 cm (36 in) square
Backing material—Homespun—92 cm (36¾ in) square plus
    seam allowance
DMC Stranded and DMC Perle 3 and 5 to tone with your
    scraps
Embroidery needles

The centre material is Homespun cotton measuring 61 cm (24 in) square. Onto the right side of this, pencil draw a wavy circle representing the stem, diameter 38 cm (15 in). Herringbone stitch this circle using DMC Perle 3. Either side of the Herringbone are Stem stitches in three strands of DMC Stranded cotton.

On a photocopier, enlarge the bow on page 26 by 172%. Trace the sewing line for the bow onto the Homespun and cut out, leaving a 1 cm (½ in) turn-under. Appliqué this bow onto the stem circle with tiny Slip stitches, turning the 'turn-under' with your needle as you sew. The flowers are selected from different patterned fabrics. Enlarge flowers and small bow on page 28 on a photocopier by 148%. Trace the patterns on the right side of the fabric and allow 1 cm (½ in) for turn-under. Appliqué these flowers on with Slip stitch in an arrangement of your choice—the illustration on page 29 is a guideline only. Leaves are placed where you feel inclined.

The work is then embellished with various stitches— these are as follows—look at the diagram as you go.

The Daisy—Buttonhole stitch with either Bullion Knots or
    French Knots in the centre.

The Rock Rose—This flower is any combination of two of the following stitches—Buttonhole, Twisted Chain, Stem, Chain and French Knots.

The Rosebud—Buttonhole, Couching and Stem stitch.

The Forget-Me-Not—(a) Stem or Twisted Chain and (b) Buttonhole

The Sunny Flower—This flower has Buttonhole stitch and Lattice Couching.

The Gumnut Baby—Lattice Couching, Cretan and Buttonhole stitch. The stamens are Couching with French Knots.

The Teardrop Bud—One row Stem stitch in one strand of DMC Perle 3 and one row Back stitch. French Knots around the outside.

The Large Bow (below)—This is Couched around the outside and a row of Back stitch is sewn up the middle of each segment.

The Leaves—These are Cretan, Fly, Feather and a combination of Buttonhole and Lazy Daisy stitch.

All stitches use a combination of DMC Perle 5 or DMC Stranded cotton in colours to complement or contrast with the fabrics you have selected. When the garland is completed, faintly draw crossing lines 5 cm (2 in) apart across the background and stitch with a tiny running or quilting stitch. This effect is called Cross-hatching.

The finished Garlanded Antimacassar (instructions start on page 25)

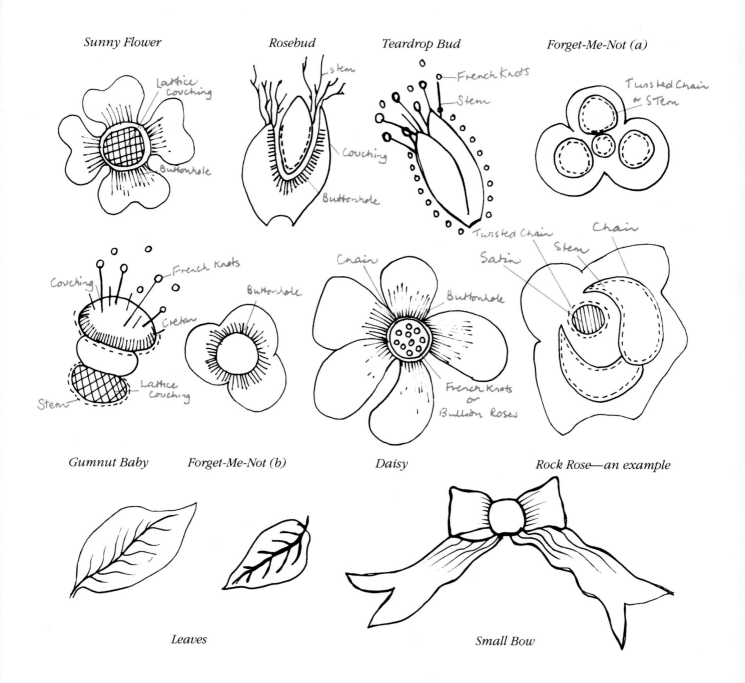

Sunny Flower *Rosebud* *Teardrop Bud* *Forget-Me-Not (a)*

Gumnut Baby *Forget-Me-Not (b)* *Daisy* *Rock Rose—an example*

Leaves *Small Bow*

THE MITRED BORDER

A mitred border 90 cm x 13 cm (36 in x 5¼ in) is then added (see diagram on page 30). To do this, centre the border strip on each side of the top to extend 15 cm (6 in) equally at each end. Use pins to mark the centres and ends of the border strips, and the centre of each edge of the top. Matching these centres, pin the borders in place. Sew on the borders, beginning and ending the stitching at the seam lines, not at the outer edge of the top. At one corner smooth one border over an adjacent one and with a pencil draw a diagonal line from

Outline in Stem

Herringbone

the inner seam line to the point where the outer edges of the two borders cross. Now reverse the two borders so the bottom one is now on the top and again draw a diagonal line as before. Matching the two pencil lines, sew them together. Cut away the excess and press the seam open. Repeat this for the other corners of the antimacassar.

For the next step see the instructions 'Attaching Batting and Backing—Basting' on page 36. The backing of Homespun is then turned to the front and neatly slip stitched around, making a border surround of 2 cm (1 in).

The Garlanded Antimacassar in the barn (instructions start on page 25)

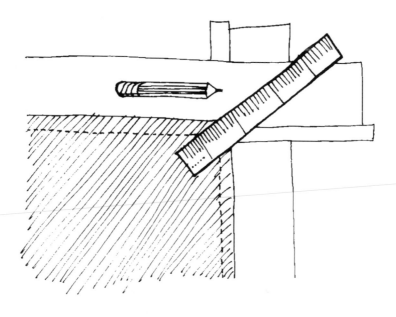

Mitring a corner

THE POULTRY QUILT

This quilt sits comfortably on a double bed. It could also be used as a rug for the back of a couch or as a decorative wall quilt. The embroidery instructions given are for the rooster and two hens centrepiece but any animal or bird would be fine. This is not a precious formal quilt—it is meant to have a casual feel and be a bit rustic-looking. The pieced blocks of the quilt are based on an old English pattern from a quilt which commemorated the Duke of Wellington's victory at the Battle of Vittoria in 1813. Gail first saw this block on a card sent from the Victoria and Albert Museum. In the USA this pattern is called Mill Wheel and we have also seen it named Vine of Friendship, Snowball and Rob Peter to Pay Paul. The Provençal material scraps were used to give an earthy, rich effect. Here are lengthy instructions on how to make a quilt—they can be used as a reference for making other quilts in this book or for your own designs.

MATERIALS REQUIRED:

Scraps of material—each 20 cm (8 in) square
Homespun for centre—32 cm (12¾ in)
Homespun in 3 different colours for borders—1 piece 56 cm (5½ in) and 2 pieces 15 cm (6 in)
Material for backing—174 cm (69½ in) square
A plait of sewing threads in various colours
Quilting thread
Your choice of DMC Stranded cotton, DMC Perle 3, DMC Perle 5 and DMC Stranded Variegated cotton
Plastic for template
Quilting needles—'betweens'
A quilting frame
Batting from a quilt shop—179 cm (71½ in) square

Quilt measures 174 cm (69½ in) square

THE APPLIQUÉD AND EMBROIDERED CENTREPIECE

The finished size of the centrepiece is 30 cm (12 in) square.

Enlarge chooks A, B and C on a photocopier by 172%. Trace the drawings onto the right side of the patterned pieces chosen for appliqué. Cut 1 cm (½ in) out from this outline. Where there are awkward corners, take a small snip into within a thread of the sewing line.

These chooks are appliquéd onto the Homespun using a small Slip stitch, turning under with the needle as you sew.

The Foraging Hen

Buttonhole stitch around the outside of the hen in three strands of DMC Stranded cotton.

Couch around the combs using DMC Perle 3.

The wing tips have rows of Fly stitch in DMC Perle 5 in parallel lines halfway down the wings. The base of the wing is encrusted with Lazy Daisy stitches in DMC Perle 3, Herring-bone in DMC Perle 5 and, over the top, Herringbone in one thread of DMC Stranded cotton. Stitch these at random using your imagination.

Stem stitch the legs and feet in DMC Perle 3.

Fly stitch the beak together in DMC Perle 3.

The Strutting Chook

Buttonhole stitch around the outside of the chook in three strands of DMC Stranded cotton.

Couch around the chook's combs in DMC Perle 3.

Sew single rows of Fly stitch at random on the wings, in DMC Stranded cotton. Inside the Fly stitch on the wings, stitch a Lazy Daisy using three strands of DMC Stranded cotton. Still on the wings, Herringbone stitch at random over the other two stitches using one strand of DMC Stranded cotton.

The feet and beak are the same as those of the Foraging Hen.

The Cocky Rooster

Stem stitch the outline using two threads of DMC Stranded cotton.

Couch the combs using DMC Perle 3. The feet are as for the hens. The jowl is Satin stitched in DMC Perle 5.

The wing tip half of the wing has rows of different coloured Fly stitch in DMC Perle 5 and one row of Fly stitch in DMC Stranded cotton. The base of the wing is Buttonhole stitched in loops with a Lazy Daisy stitch and a French Knot in each loop. These stitches are designed to give a feathery effect.

THE WELLINGTON BLOCK QUILT TOP

In all, 32 blocks 20 cm (8 in) square are sewn together. Before cutting, wash your material to check it is colourfast and preshrunk.

Templates

The templates for this quilt are given in correct size on page 33. To make templates trace carefully over the pattern piece. Trace this pattern onto a stiff plastic which will retain a sharp edge. Cut out the two pieces accurately with a Stanley knife.

Cutting the Pieces

Lay your fabric on a smooth surface with the wrong side up. The template is shown without the 5 mm (¼ in) seam allowance which you will have to allow room for when tracing your pattern onto the material. Always place the template so that as many straight sides as possible are parallel with the grain of the material. Mark with a sharp lead pencil. This is the sewing line and must be accurate.

Measure 5 mm (¼ in) around this shape and draw a line. This is the line you will cut on. Continue moving the templates and tracing them onto the material the required number of times—128 of template X and 128 of template Y. You will save fabric if pieces share a common cutting line.

Sewing the Block by Hand

Place two pieces together, right sides facing (X facing Y) and pin through both pieces at one end of the pencil line. On all the rounded corners snip slightly into the 5 mm (¼ in) seam allowance so that when sewn the fabric sits flat. Stitch exactly on the pencil line starting at the unpinned end. Use a short needle and not more than 45 cm (18 in) of thread. Join the pieces with short running stitches. Press the seams lightly.

It is important with this Wellington Block pattern to balance the colours well—have light colours opposite each other. Once you have sewn each X and Y together to make a square you can then sew together your 20 cm (8 in) squares, or

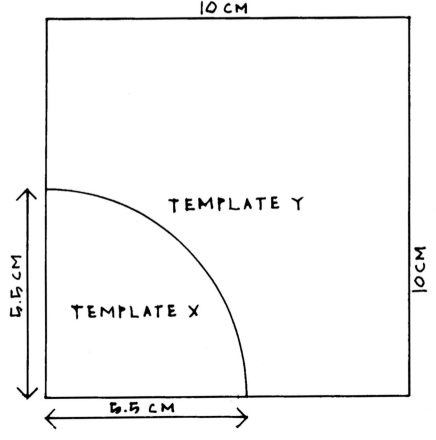

The corner chicks from the Poultry Quilt (instructions start on page 31)

'blocks' as they are called, by joining four squares together with the X sections meeting to form a circle. Be sure your centrepoint is accurate.

Joining the Blocks

After you have pieced the 32 blocks, lay them out and jiggle them around to create the final effect. Using the 5 mm (¼ in) seam allowance join the blocks in horizontal rows. Join two rows together, always matching seam lines, then add other rows. When crossing seam lines be careful to match seam to seam. Where you are joining a long row, pin each side of each seam so you know the seams will be accurate when you sew.

ADDING BORDERS

The first border is four pieces of border material 14 cm x 120 cm (5½ in x 48 in). Measure this size onto the wrong side of the fabric and draw a sewing line. Allow 5 mm (¼ in) all around for the seam allowance. Using the 5 mm (¼ in) seam allowance attach the borders to each side of the joined blocks. Sew in four contrasting coloured corners 14 cm (5½ in) square.

The second border is made up of two plain materials, each 3.75 cm (1½ in) wide and 148 cm (59¼ in) long with 5 mm (¼ in) seam allowances. Join these two together, then sew onto the first border, leaving the corners vacant.

The finished Poultry Quilt

THE CORNER CHICKENS IN REVERSE APPLIQUÉ

The chicks in the corner are created by reverse appliqué. In this process the shape is revealed after a section of the top material is cut away to expose a layer of fabric underneath. Reverse appliqué makes small pieces easier to handle and gives the perception of depth instead of the stacking effect of ordinary appliqué.

Enlarge D on a photocopier by 172%. Make the template for the chickens by tracing D and transferring to a piece of plastic.

Both the inner and outer materials are 11 cm (4¼ in) square finished, so cut 13 cm (5¼ in) squares of fabric. Tack the top plain fabric to the patterned fabric underneath and lightly trace around the chicken template on the plain fabric.

Pierce the fabric at the centre of the design with sharp scissors and cut away the excess material in the centre leaving 5 mm (¼ in) inside the line as a turn-under allowance. Snip into the curves and corners within a thread of the pencil line so they will sit well (see photograph at bottom of page 38). Turn the fabric under and finger press it along the pencil line; slip stitch the fabrics neatly together.

The outline is sewn with Feather stitch in two threads of DMC Stranded Variegated cotton. The legs are Herringbone stitch in two threads of DMC Stranded cotton. The claws are Stem stitch in the same cotton and the beak is Satin stitch in two threads of DMC Stranded cotton. The eyes are blue French Knots with white Lazy Daisy stitching around in one thread of DMC Stranded cotton. The eye is outlined in one thread of black DMC Stranded cotton and sewn with Stem stitch.

This corner square is then sewn into the border and Buttonhole stitched around with three threads of DMC Variegated Stranded cotton.

MARKING THE QUILTING PATTERN

Because this quilt is already quite complex, it is best quilted with simple Cross-hatching. Mark all quilting lines with a soft 6B lead pencil on the right side of the material starting in the centre with a diagonal line from corner to corner. Then place lines 7 cm (2¾ in) out from this centre line. Criss-cross all of the quilt. The plain blue border has a tramline quilting pattern and the red border on the very outside has a small diamond pattern drawn on with a stencil from a quilting shop.

ATTACHING BATTING AND BACKING—BASTING

The material for backing the quilt should be a soft, good quality cotton which should be washed. The batting, or middle layer, can be bought from a quilt shop and should be cut 5 cm (2 in) larger than the quilt top, as should the backing material. Place

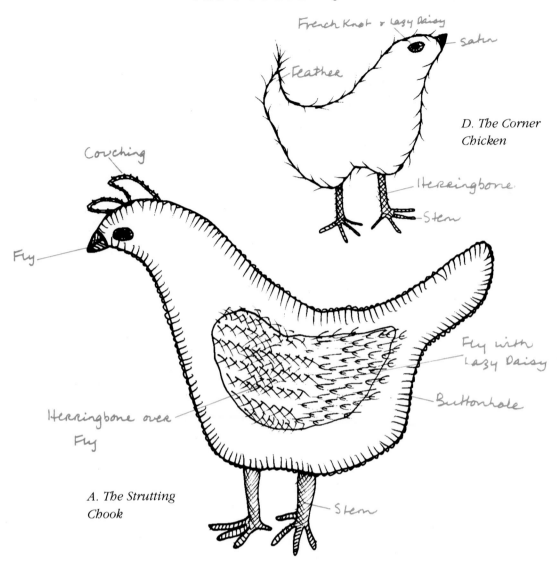

French Knot & Lazy Daisy

Satin

Feather

D. The Corner Chicken

Couching

Herringbone

Fly

Stem

Fly with Lazy Daisy

Buttonhole

Herringbone over Fly

A. The Strutting Chook

Stem

the backing wrong side up on a flat surface. Place the batting on top of this, matching the outer edges. Now, centre the quilt top right side up on top of the batting. Flatten the three layers carefully. Baste (another word for sew) the three layers together by first stretching the fabric flat and pinning the layers together. Baste with long—5 cm (2 in)—stitches, starting in the centre and sewing toward the edges in diagonal lines. The rows of basting lines should be as close as 8 cm (3¼ in) apart. You baste the quilt to keep it flat and together during the quilting period. After quilting, these basting stitches are removed.

QUILTING

It is important to remember that you always start quilting from the centre of your quilt outwards. This ensures there will be no puckering. The actual quilting stitch is a fairly simple one. The stitch is a tiny running stitch working through the three layers at once. It is best to push the needle vertically all the way through the three layers and then push it back in what are two separate movements.

The Poultry Quilt under the cypresses (instructions start on page 31)

The rooster and two hens centrepiece on the Poultry Quilt

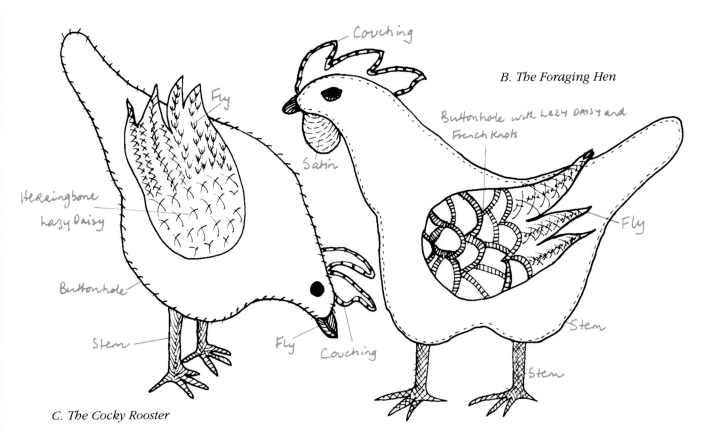

Couching

B. The Foraging Hen

Fly

Buttonhole with Lazy Daisy and French Knots

Herringbone

Lazy Daisy

Satin

Buttonhole

Fly

Stem

Fly

Couching

Stem

Stem

C. The Cocky Rooster

Use a short, fine needle designed for quilting called a 'betweens' and 100 per cent cotton quilting thread. Using a quilting hoop gives a better finish to your quilting. Place the hoop over the middle of the quilt, pull the quilt taut and move extra fullness to the edges. Begin in the centre and quilt outwards.

Begin with a 45 cm (18 in) length of thread with a knot in one end. Insert the needle into the quilt through the top about 1 cm (½ in) from where you plan to begin quilting and bring the needle up to the quilting line. Pull gently but firmly, and bury the knot in the layer of batting. Now place your left hand under the hoop where the needle should come through. Use this hand to feel when the needle has penetrated the three layers.

Small stitches are ideal, however, the even length of stitches and spaces is more important. Do not quilt right to the edge of the quilt top, as you will need to turn the edges under when you 'butt' them. When the entire quilt top has been quilted, remove the basting stitches. This is an exciting move.

The final job is to 'butt' the edge of the quilt. Turn the backing fabric and the quilt top edge in and sew small quilting stitches just in from the edge.

THE SUNSHINE QUILT

This quilt married together various ideas which evolved during our weekly chats on projects for this book. The blue and white blocks were inspired by a piece of china from the rubbish tip on our property, Craigton. The overall plan of the quilt was to create a South of France feeling and the sun centre seemed the best way of doing this. The finished quilt is perfect for a single bed and will freshen any room.

MATERIALS REQUIRED:

Blue fabric—150 cm (60 in)
Red border material—50 cm (20 in)
White fabric—200 cm (80 in)
Orange fabric—20 cm (8 in)
Yellow fabric—20 cm (8 in)
Quilting thread in blue and sewing threads
Plastic for templates
Batting—137 cm (54¾ in) wide and 183 cm (73¼ in) long
Yellow check backing fabric—137 cm (54¾ in) wide and
    183 cm (73¼ in) long
DMC Perle 5—black and white

Quilt measures 175 cm x 130 cm (70 in x 52 in)

CUTTING THE MATERIAL FOR THE CENTRE PANEL

To make the centre panel mark three pieces of blue fabric to these dimensions on the wrong side:

a) One square 39 cm x 39 cm (15½ in x 15½ in)
b) Two rectangles 39 cm x 20 cm (15½ in x 8 in)

Add a 5 mm (¼ in) seam allowance and cut the three out. The red border of the centre is then marked:

a) Two pieces 3 cm x 90 cm (1¼ in x 36 in), and
b) Four pieces 3 cm x 39 cm (1¼ in x 15½ in)

These are cut out, again allowing a 5 mm (¼ in) seam allowance. Enlarge the sun illustration on page 43 on a photocopier by 172%. Trace the individual shapes of the illustration onto the right side of your yellow, white, orange and red fabric. Cut these shapes allowing 5 mm (¼ in) for turning under.

APPLIQUÉ

The sun face is four different layers of appliqué. Start by appliquéing the yellow centre onto the orange circle. The

orange and yellow are then appliquéd onto the white and then onto the red material. Use the appliqué technique suggested for the Garlanded Antimacassar, using tiny Slip stitches.

EMBROIDERY

The stitching details of the sun are sewn before it is appliquéd onto the centre blue panel. The eyes, mouth and outline of the yellow middle are stitched in Twisted Chain stitch in black DMC Perle 5.

The centre of the eye is Satin stitch in white DMC Perle 5. The white rays are outlined using black DMC Perle 5 in Interlaced Chain stitch. The yellow outer circle is outlined in two lines of Couching using black DMC Perle 5, 1.5 cm (¾ in) apart. The black dots outside the circle are three stitches of Satin stitch in black DMC Perle 5.

ASSEMBLING THE CENTRE PANEL

To assemble the centre panel, sew the four short pieces of red border to the long sides of each blue rectangle. Then sew the top side and the bottom side of the blue sun square to the red border on one side of each rectangle. Add the two long, red side borders to the three connected blue pieces to complete the panel.

CUTTING OUT THE QUILT BLOCKS

Make templates by tracing the templates on pages 44 and 46 onto stiff plastic, cutting these out carefully. On the wrong side of the fabric draw the sewing line against the template edge and measure the cutting line 5 mm (¼ in) out on every piece,

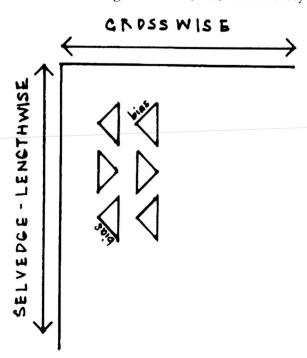

Fig. A
Suggested cutting plan which has the long side of the ½ square triangles on the straight grain of the fabric

as instructed in 'Cutting the Pieces' in the Poultry Quilt directions on page 33. The longest sides of the triangular pieces should be on the straight grain of the fabric. This is important when you have half blocks edging the quilt as the long edge can stretch. Use a cutting plan as in Fig. A, remembering always to add 5 mm (¼ in) for seam allowance.

Trace and cut:
112 of template A on to the white material
123 of template B on to the blue material
17 of template C on to the white material
17 of template D on to the white material
35 of template E on to the blue material
11 of template F on to the white material
11 of template G on to the white material

In the corner of the template A material, snip into the sewing line to within a thread—see Fig. B on page 45.

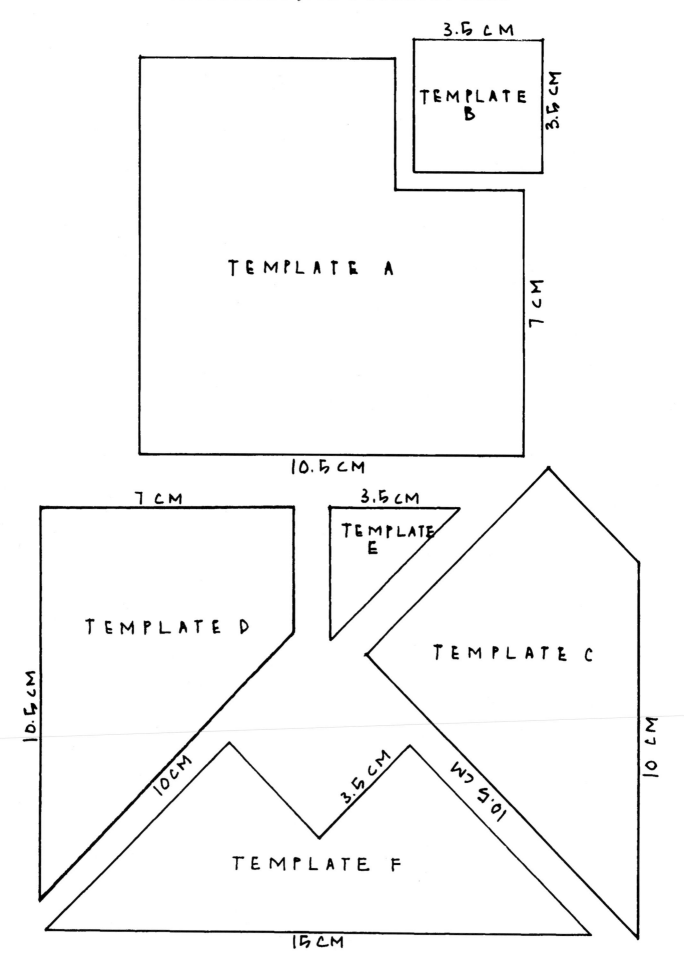

The Sunshine Quilt in the lavender (instructions start on page 40)

SEWING THE BLOCKS

Sew each individual block—169 in all. Refer to 'Sewing the Block by Hand' in the Poultry Quilt instructions on page 33.

JOINING THE BLOCKS TOGETHER

A quilt with diagonally set blocks is just as easy to join as one with blocks set horizontally. The only difference for this

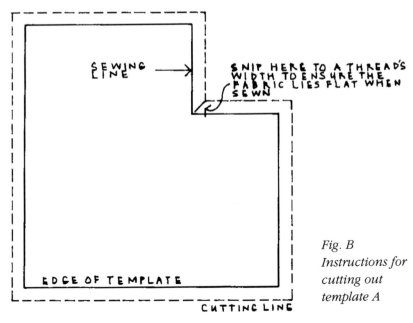

SEWING LINE

SNIP HERE TO A THREAD'S WIDTH TO ENSURE THE FABRIC LIES FLAT WHEN SEWN

EDGE OF TEMPLATE

CUTTING LINE

Fig. B Instructions for cutting out template A

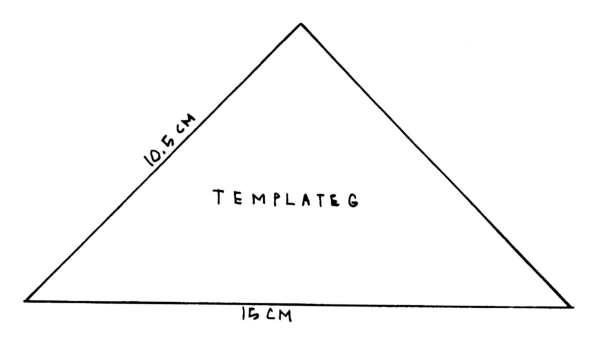

diagonal set is that you must add half squares to fill in the edges around the centrepiece and around the outside. Refer back to 'Joining the Blocks' in the Poultry Quilt directions on page 34. It is easier to join the corners that are independent of the centre panel first and then to join blocks to the side of the centre panel and work out from the sides. Finally, join these to the corners.

ADDING THE BORDER

The border is added using straight rather than mitred corners. See 'Adding Borders' in the Poultry Quilt on page 34.

MARKING THE QUILTING PATTERN

This quilt is marked with Cross-hatching across the white blocks: faintly draw crossing lines 5 cm (2 in) apart across the blocks and stitch with a tiny running or quilting stitch. In the centre panel, circular quilting lines are repeated three times outside the black dots. These are drawn freehand. The other two blue panels are closely Cross-hatched as above.

ATTACHING BATTING AND BACKING

Follow the directions in the Poultry Quilt on page 36—they are the same for all quilts.

QUILTING

Follow the marked pattern with even running stitch as for the Poultry Quilt on page 37. Remember to start at the centre and always work outwards. We added blue piping to the edge to bring the blue out from the centre. The backing and quilt top or front are 'butted' and small Slip stitches join it together.

THE SUNFLOWER TABLEMATS

Sunflowers are synonymous with summer. In the paddocks nearby, the large heads follow the sun in a daily swing. Gail grew them last summer en masse in her vegetable garden and Debo and I wished we had too when we saw them for sale for $3.50 a stem in city florist shops. I had minor doubts about our use of sunflowers, believing that by the time the book was published they would be passé in decorating circles. Then I decided they were timeless—Van Gogh's are firmly imprinted in our consciousness and besides, the sunflowers aptly continue our Provençal theme.

For these tablemats a thick, twill cotton was chosen. The twill is a close weave to hold the embroidery threads and yet is easy to sew through. Use a light box to trace the pattern onto the material.

MATERIALS REQUIRED:

Cotton twill fabric—1 m (3 ft)
DMC Perle 5—3362, 501, 3345, 725, 726 and 772
DMC Stranded cotton—3371
DMC Soft cotton 2726 and 2732
Ginnie Thompson Flower threads—310 and 350
Soie Crystale silk—green

THE RELUCTANT SUNFLOWER

Enlarge illustration on page 48 on a photocopier by 122%. Trace onto the cotton twill fabric.

Starting in the centre of the flower, the sepal is worked in four threads of Soie Crystale silk. An alternative thread is DMC Perle 5—3362. The stitch is Split Back stitch and this stitch is also continued down the stem. The outer calyx is worked in Satin stitch using DMC Perle 5—501.

The open bud is worked in green DMC Perle 5—3345 in Roumanian Couching. When stitching each section of the green bud, stitch the first row down the centre of the segment, and subsequent rows paralleling this first row. This may become clearer if you look at the detailing on the drawing. This Roumanian Couching gives a leaf-like, textured effect.

The petals are worked the same way as the bud leaves in Roumanian Couching, alternating two yellows of DMC Perle 5—725 and 726.

Between some of the petals Stem stitch is worked in one strand of DMC Stranded cotton—3371 to give the flower a three-dimensional look.

*The Reluctant
Sunflower
(instructions on
page 47)*

Satin

Roumanian
couching

Stem

split back

*The Full Bloom
Sunflower
(instructions on
page 50)*

Roumanian Couching

Fly

French Knots

French Knots with
open Herringbone
over the top

Split Back

Back

Whipped Stem

Turkey Work

THE FULL BLOOM SUNFLOWER

Enlarge illustration on page 49 on a photocopier by 122%. Trace onto the cotton twill fabric.

The centre is encrusted French Knots using three threads of green Soie Crystale silk. Two outer lines of this centre are French Knots in a paler green—DMC Perle 5—772. Over these pale green knots open Herringbone stitches are worked in yellow Ginnie Thompson Flower thread—310.

The seed casings are rows of orange Ginnie Thompson Flower thread—350 in Fly stitch starting at the outside line and working to the centre. See the drawing for the detailing. This procedure is repeated, encircling the centre. Then dark brown Back stitches are sewn in rows to resemble seeds, in two threads of DMC Stranded cotton—3371.

The next ring of the flower is three rows of Turkey Work stitch using both yellow DMC Soft cotton—2726, and khaki DMC Soft cotton—2732 in the same needle. This gives the soft, brushy effect the sunflower has if you look closely.

The base of each petal is worked in Roumanian Couching in DMC Perle 5 thread—725. The rest of each petal is sewn in Roumanian Couching in yellow DMC Perle 5—726.

The green in between the petals is worked in Split Back stitch using green Soie Crystale silk. Between all petals one thread of orange Ginnie Thompson Flower thread—350 is also used in Stem stitch. Sometimes the Stem stitch is whipped with one or two threads of brown DMC Stranded cotton—3371. These special effects give dimension and subtlety to the petals. Plain black stitching would be too dense.

CURTAIN KEEPERS

These keepers, or tie-backs, are designed for plain curtains such as calico; they give a touch of style simply and easily to a humble fabric. We had in mind a simple project for an apartment dweller, a first home owner or a beach house owner. Try them for seaside cottage curtains and don't be daunted by the sound of Interlaced Chain stitch; it's not that difficult.

THE AIX-EN-PROVENCE KEEPER

MATERIALS REQUIRED:

Les Olivades fabric or similar—25 cm (10 in)
DMC Stranded cottons of your choice
Natural Homespun—25 cm (10 in)
Soft dacron cord
Large needle for threading cord

Enlarge illustration on page 54 on a photocopier by 141% and make two copies. Cut out the two templates, A and B. On to a 25 cm (10 in) piece of Les Olivades fabric which has been doubled over, place template A onto the fold of the fabric and trace around it. Cut out, allowing 5 mm (¼ in) seam allowance all around. Repeat this step so that you have two identical pieces. Trace template B onto the natural Homespun. Trace the pattern to be worked onto the inside of the Homespun. The embroidery is then worked in stitches illustrated on the diagram using three threads of DMC Stranded cotton. The Homespun is then cut out, leaving 5 mm (¼ in) seam allowance. It is then slip stitched onto the Les Olivades fabric with inconspicuous sewing thread.

The back and front of the Les Olivades materials are sewn together either by hand or by machine, right sides together. They are then turned inside out. Use a small running stitch around the outside of the Homespun, making sure you sew both Les Olivades layers together. The outside casing is then stuffed with a soft dacron cord drawn through using a large needle.

THE TARTAN KEEPER

The stitches used on this second keeper give the effect of a rich braid. These are stitch combinations which can be used for a number of projects, especially where joins need to be hidden.

☞ p 54

The Tartan Keeper (instructions on page 54)

The Aix-en-Provence Keeper (instructions on page 51)

Opposite: The Aix-en-Provence Keeper on a calico curtain in the barn

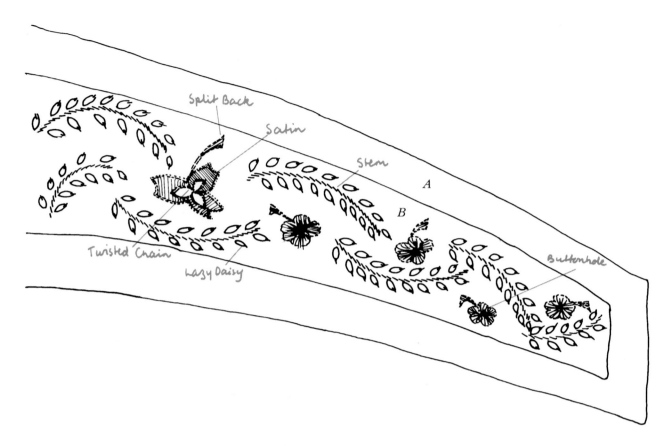

MATERIALS REQUIRED:

Tartan fabric—25 cm (10 in)
A fabric to match the tartan—25 cm (10 in)
Soft dacron cord
Large needle for threading cord
DMC Stranded cotton and DMC Perle 5 in colours
    complementing your fabrics

Enlarge the illustration on a photocopier by 172% and make
two copies. Cut out the two templates, A and B. Place template
A onto the fold of the doubled-over piece of matching fabric
(we used a starry fabric), then trace around the template.
Repeat this step so that you have two identical pieces. Trace
template B onto the tartan fabric and cut out. The tartan fabric
is sewn onto the matching fabric and the embroidery is then
worked in rows:

Row 1: Stem stitch with six threads DMC Stranded cotton
Row 2: Interlaced Chain stitch in DMC Perle 5 in
            contrasting colours
Row 3: Repeat first row
Row 4: Satin stitch in DMC Perle 5
Row 5: Back stitch in DMC Perle 5

The keeper is then made up according to the the Aix-en-
Provence Keeper instructions. Tartan piping is used to edge
the keeper.

ROSIE'S BRAIDED CUSHION

This project involves sewing rows of stitches to produce individual braids of your own texture and colour. It is a good project to practise your stitching for more ambitious projects. Once you learn to sew your own braid you can create stylish cushions from inexpensive fabrics, from expensive remnants or from a mix of both. Great treasures can be found by fossicking in the remnant baskets of various shops.

For our cushion (see photographs overleaf) we combined a piece of Provençal border we had tucked away, with a tartan remnant. To buy the braid would have been impossible, so we sewed our own with rows of stitches in complementary colours. In the instructions here we do not mention colours, as we imagine you choosing your own.

Start with the middle row of stitches in the braid, which effectively covers the seam of the two materials. This is sewn with Herringbone stitch in DMC Soft cotton. These stitches should be about 8 mm (⅓ in) wide. For the next row in towards the centre of the cushion, lightly draw a line 5 mm (¼ in) out from the Herringbone stitch as a gauge for a row of Satin stitch in DMC Perle 3. The next row inward is a single row of Stem stitch in DMC Perle 3.

Now move to the outside of the middle Herringbone row for a row of Chain stitch using three threads of DMC Stranded cotton. Then, edging outwards, a row of Stem stitch in DMC Perle 5. Next, a row of Chain stitch in two threads of DMC Stranded cotton.

Using the different thicknesses of threads gives the braid more texture and interest and puts your stamp on it. Braid stitch used in this way can be effective edging for dinner mats, seat covers, serviettes and guest hand towels.

*Rosie's Braided
Cushion
(instructions on
page 55)*

*Detail of the
stitched braid on
Rosie's Braided
Cushion*

CHAPTER ❧ THREE

TREASURES FROM THE TIP

The inspirations for the needlework designs in this chapter come directly from a settler's tip on Debo's property, Yallambi, halfway between Maude and Anakie in Victoria. In typically enthusiastic style, Debo decided her birthday treat would be a 'dig' in what was suspected to be the remnants of a tip. Duncan had seen the glint of broken glass in the grass a few weeks earlier. This particular tip is watched over by a single hawthorn tree and dwarf iris, the last reminders of former life. In the same area are the remains of a shepherd's hut with the stone-paved floor of a sheepfold. The shepherds of the Yallambi hills must have led a spartan, isolated life with few material possessions, however, a few finds suggest some decorative indulgences. Most of the broken pieces revealed by the dig were Blue and White Transfer Printed Earthenware from around the 1830s. A Wild Rose pattern piece from Middlesbrough Pottery was second in popularity to the Willow Pattern in Great Britain, however, used as a design for today's needlework it throws off its common connotations and becomes quite special.

Our property Craigton is also ideal for earthenware rummaging, for in the 1850s, the Moorabool Viaduct was built over the river here. While the bluestone bridge was being constructed a village of sorts sprang up along the river and so we have found blue and white bits from the 1830s here too.

The footstool, box lid and brick shown here are designs from the finds of our tips, while the Carlton Quilt comes from an old tessellated verandah floor in the Melbourne suburb of Carlton. These designs may spark the same inquisitiveness in others to look at private tips on old properties through different eyes.

THE WILD ROSE BOX

This might be a box for treasures, but after you have made it, you will surely call it your treasured box. This is a challenging project.

MATERIALS REQUIRED:

Natural Homespun—38 cm x 32 cm (15¼ in x 12¾ in)
DMC Stranded cotton—755, 677, 613, 798 and 3032
DMC Perle 3—797, 755, 677, 832 and 725
DMC Perle 5—755, 932, 725, 676, 677, 729, 334, 3722 and 752
Quilting thread—stone-coloured
Watercolours threads—Autumn Leaves and Buttercup
1 sheet of heavy cardboard from an art supply shop
1 sheet of light cardboard
Double-sided sticky tape
Stanley knife
Check cotton fabric—25 cm (10 in)
Plain cotton fabric—25 cm (10 in)
Fabric glue—optional though advisable

THE BOX LID

Enlarge box lid illustration on a photocopier by 141%. The box lid pattern and border are traced onto the piece of natural Homespun fabric using a lead pencil. The finished size of the box lid is 28 cm x 23 cm (11¼ in x 9¼ in). You should make sure the pattern is running straight on the grain of the fabric.

We have suggested colours for these flowers however we hope you will choose your own.

Little Lurking Flower

This flower is worked from the centre out.

Satin stitch in DMC Perle 3—797.

Stem stitch in DMC Perle 3—755.

Buttonhole stitch in DMC Perle 3—677.

Stem stitch in DMC Perle 3—797 whipped with two threads of DMC Stranded cotton—755.

French Knots on a tail in DMC Perle 3—677 with single French Knots in the middle.

Flying French Knot Flower

Short and Long stitch the outside of the flower in DMC Perle 5—755.

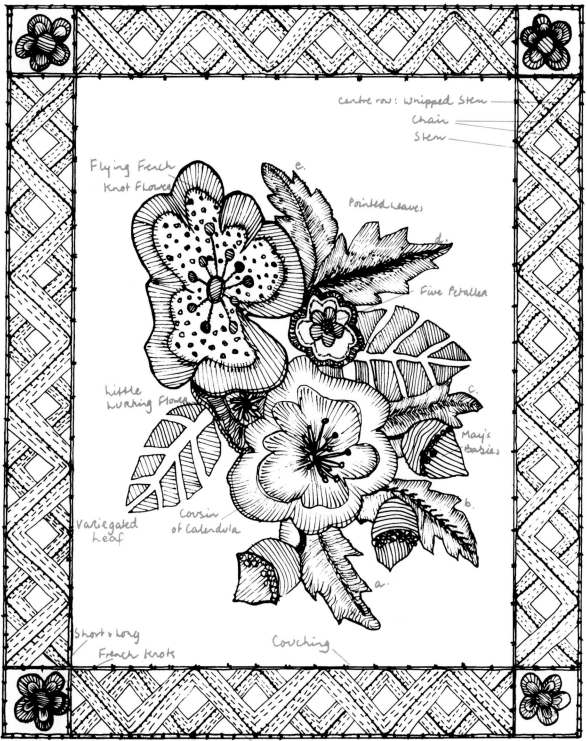

centre row: Whipped Stem

Chain

Stem

Flying French
Knot Flower

e.

Pointed Leaves

d.

Five Petaller

Little
Lurking Flower

c.

May's
Babies

b.

Variegated
Leaf

Cousin
of Calendula

a.

Short & Long
French Knots

Couching

Couching & Twisted Chain
inside Stem.

The next row of stitches is in contrasting tone toward the inside of the flower. The stitches are Short and Long in DMC Perle 5—932.

In the very centre of the flower Stem stitch around the circle, filling it in, using two strands of DMC Stranded cotton—755.

Small Satin stitch the circles and connect them to the centre circle with Stem stitch worked in two threads of DMC Stranded cotton—798.

Place French Knots in three threads of DMC Stranded cotton in various blues at random.

Cousin of Calendula

The whole flower is filled in with three rows of Short and Long stitches in DMC Perle 5 in different shades of the one colour—725, 676, 677.

The stamens are French Knots on a Tail in Watercolours thread—Autumn Leaves.

Five Petaller

Twisted Chain stitch around the outside of the flower in DMC Perle 3—677.

The next line is Chain stitch in two strands of DMC Stranded cotton—798. Close to this, Back stitch in one thread of DMC Stranded cotton—677.

Work the inside of the flower in two threads of Satin stitch outlined in Back stitch using DMC Stranded cotton—798.

Fill the centre with French Knots in DMC Stranded cotton—677.

May's Babies

Fill in the bottom of the bud with rows of Stem stitch in Watercolours threads—Autumn Leaves.

Into the top of the bud work in Satin stitch in DMC Perle 5—676 on one, and DMC Perle 5—755 on the other.

Dividing the top and bottom of the bud is a string of French Knots in DMC Perle 3—832 or 798.

Variegated Leaves

Sections of these leaves only are worked in Split Back stitch using four threads of DMC Stranded cotton—613.

Pointed Leaves

Opposite: The embroidered lid of the Wild Rose Box (instructions start on page 58)

a) The leaf outline is in Buttonhole stitch in two threads of DMC Stranded cotton—3032. Fill in from centre outwards in Satin stitch using three threads of DMC Stranded cotton—613. Twisted Chain stitch is worked

down the centre in Watercolours thread—Autumn Leaves.

b) Work Satin stitch from the outside of the leaf in four threads of DMC Stranded cotton—3032. Fly stitch is worked down the centre of the leaf in two threads of DMC Stranded cotton—613.

c) Same as (a).

d) Same as (b) but with close Fly stitch in Watercolours thread—Autumn Leaves down the centre.

e) This leaf is Buttonhole stitched around the edge using two threads of DMC Stranded cotton—613. Fill the leaf in with closed Fly stitch using four threads of DMC Stranded cotton—3032.

The Border

The centre line is Stem stitch in DMC Perle 5—729 and Whipped in 677, following a zig-zag line around the lid top.

On either side of the Stem stitch is a row of Chain stitch in DMC Perle 5—932.

The outer line is Stem stitch in two strands of DMC Stranded cotton—677.

The outside and inside edge of the box lid is Couched with Watercolours thread—Buttercup and DMC Perle 5—676.

The corner flowers are two rows of Short and Long stitch in two threads of DMC Perle 5—334 and 3722. The yellow centre is two French Knots in DMC Perle 5—752.

The extreme outside of the border is one row of Stem stitch in DMC Perle 3—725 and one row of Twisted Chain stitch in DMC Perle 5—729.

Quilting

Mark a Cross-hatch design on the lid by drawing lines lightly in pencil 2 cm (1 in) apart diagonally across the fabric. Stitch along the lines with stone-coloured quilting thread using a running stitch. A piece of sheeting used as a lining gives the lid a bit of body before it is quilted.

MAKING THE BOX

This is fairly complicated to explain so you will have to bear with us. The result is satisfying and worth the perseverance. A photograph of a complete box appears on page 86, the Wattle Box.

Cutting Out the Card

As you cut these out, number them on the back.

1. Box lid top and base of box—2 pieces 23 cm x 28 cm (9¼ in x 11¼ in) of heavy card.

2. Box lid sides—2 pieces 23 cm x 4 cm (9¼ in x 1½ in) of heavy card.

3. Box lid sides—2 pieces 28 cm x 4 cm (11¼ in x 1½ in) of heavy card.

4. Box bottom sides—2 pieces 23 cm x 6 cm (9¼ in x 2½ in) of heavy card.

5. Box bottom sides—2 pieces 28 cm x 6 cm (11¼ in x 2½ in) of heavy card.

6. Lid lining and base of box lining—2 pieces 22.5 cm x 27.5 cm (9 in x 11 in) of light card.

7. Box sides lining—2 pieces 27.5 cm x 7 cm (11 in x 2¾ in) of light card.

8. Box sides lining—2 pieces 22.5 cm x 7 cm (9 in x 2¾ in) of light card.

Cutting Out the Material

As you cut out fabric, number each piece on the wrong side.

9. Box base in check—1 piece 26 cm x 31 cm (10½ in x 12½ in)

10. Box lid sides in check—2 pieces 26 cm x 12 cm (10½ in x 4¾ in)

11. Box lid sides in check—2 pieces 33 cm x 12 cm (13¼ in x 4¾ in)

12. Box bottom sides in check—2 pieces 28 cm x 12 cm (11¼ in x 4¾ in)

13. Box bottom sides in check—2 pieces 32 cm x 12 cm (12¾ in x 4¾ in)

14. Box lid lining and base lining in plain—2 pieces 26 cm x 32 cm (10½ in x 12¾ in)

15. Box sides lining in plain—2 pieces 15 cm x 32 cm (6 in x 12¾ in)

16. Box sides lining in plain—2 pieces 15 cm x 28 cm (6 in x 11¼ in)

Making the Box Lid

Centre the embroidered piece on the first Card 1, keeping the grain straight with the edge. Lace across one way, tighten slightly and tie off the cotton thread. Repeat the lacing the other way. See Fig. C.

To make the lid sides, Cards 2 are wrapped by Fabrics 10, and Cards 3 are wrapped by Fabrics 11. Crease the fabric in half lengthways. Put double-sided sticky tape on one long edge of the card. Place that taped long edge along the centre crease of the fabric. See Fig. D. Fold in the short ends of the fabric. Fold the main fabric over the top and pin firmly along the long edge of the card. Sew small, tight running stitches where the pins are or machine along using 'zipper foot', stitching tight up to the card. Repeat for all four sides of the box lid.

Take one short and one long side and with the ends together and with the fold facing outward, Slip stitch together the fabric

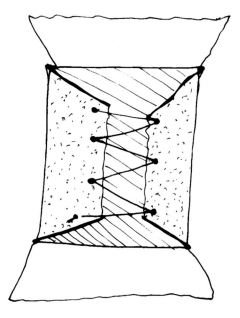

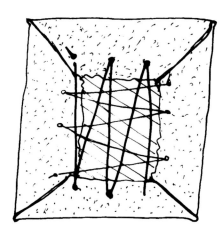

Fig. C. Lacing your embroidered top onto Card 1

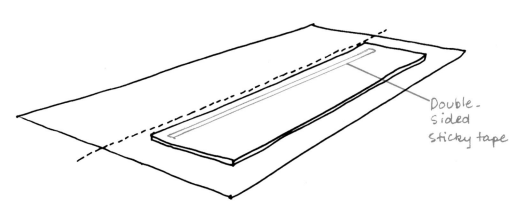

Double-sided sticky tape

Fig. D. Making the lid sides

which is covering the cardboard. This is done to three corners of the box lid and should result in neat outside corners. Now you are ready for the fourth side, to make a 'square'. Sew these last two together with the sides where the material covers the cardboard facing you. The sides with the folded-over fabric are always on the inside of the lid.

Slip stitch the box lid to the sides, holding it firm with long pins in the corner as you sew. The folded edge is on the bottom or inside of the box lid. The lid is finished with Couching in DMC Perle 3 and DMC Perle 5. This Couching hides the overstitching on the corners. You can, however, leave it bare or use braid.

Making the Box Bottom

It is easiest to start with the sides. Cover Cards 4 with Fabrics 12 and Cards 5 with Fabrics 13 using two lengths of double-sided sticky tape on the card to keep the fabric in place. Fold in the short ends of the fabric. Run a piece of the tape

The Wild Rose Box lid (instructions start on page 58, see page 86 for photograph of a complete box)

lengthways along the short edges of the fabric and fold the fabric to the centre. Join the corners as you did for the lid sides. For the base of the box, cover the second Card 1 with Fabric 9 using the same procedure as with the sides. Assemble as with lid sides and lid top, or Slip stitch base to bottom sides, holding with long pins in the corners while you sew.

Lid Lining and Base Lining

Wrap the lid lining and base lining, Cards 6 with Fabrics 14, the same as for the box bottom. Stick with the tape. Slip into the lid and base after cutting any excess corner fabric of the lid top away in a 'V'. If these look at all loose, paste with craft glue.

Rising Linings

Wrap Cards 7 and 8 with Fabrics 15 and 16 using the double-sided sticky tape method. These do not have to be sewn as they are just placed in the box. If you wish you can apply fabric glue inside the top edge of the box sides, pegging as you glue.

THE POPPY ROSE FOOTSTOOL

MATERIALS REQUIRED:

Irish twill linen—50 cm (20 in) square
Appletons wools—blues—741, 742, 745, pinks—751, 753, 754, greens—294, 293, 352, 401, yellow—471

Enlarge illustration on a photocopier by 172%. Trace the pattern onto the linen using a light box. The entire work is stitched in Appletons wools (see photograph on page 68).

a) The Centre Rose

Work in Short and Long stitch in two shades of pink, with the centre of the rose in very pale pink. Each petal is one row of Short and Long stitch in dark pink starting at the top of the petal. The second row is light pink working from the base of the petal back into the first row.

b) Meconopsis (poppy)

Work each petal separately in Short and Long stitch. The first row is in pale blue, the second row in deeper blue and the third in dark blue. Buttonhole stitch around the inside, working the yellow thread into the dark blue.

All four poppies use the same technique with different combinations of the three blues. All stems are pale green Stem stitch. Use more rows to make thicker stems.

c) Leaves

Work the outside of the leaves first in Short and Long Buttonhole stitch in dark green. Work the insides in Fly stitch using a paler green and working into the Buttonhole stitches.

d) Leaves

These leaves you should work in the reverse colours to (c).

e) Leaves

Work these leaves in Fly stitch using combinations of pale and dark green colours.

f) Dark Little Flower

Work the petals in Split Back stitch. Yellow Fly stitches come to a point—see drawing.

g) Rosebuds

Work in shades of pink using rows of Split Back stitch.

h) Leaves

Work these leaves in green Split Back stitch.

i) Seedpods

These seedpods are rows of Split Back stitch using two shades
of green. Work the top round knob in Satin stitch.

THE CARLTON QUILT

Though many of the designs in quiltmaking are considered 'pioneer American' or 'classically British' it is as well to realise that few quiltmakers' designs are entirely isolated from a combination of images which are handed down and possess a sense of the past. For example, the 'Mariner's Compass', a familiar quilting pattern, is a reflection of early Grecian tiles. We see 'quilting' designs with every step we take—tessellated tiled Victorian floors in the Melbourne suburb of Carlton, Mediterranean wall tile patterns at a garden design exhibition, exquisite ceilings in boom-time mansions and even the pattern of the freshly cut lucerne in our valley paddock; each allows us to reflect on the universality of images and their collective influence, as well as suggesting ideas for quilting.

It is with these musings in mind that we decided to use some tessellated tiles in a quilt. Some floors are fairly simple and would be ideal for a first attempt at 'piecing'. The design we chose has a decorative flower which lends itself to embroidery. On the floor this feature is white but we decided to feature it as a change of texture on the quilt instead.

This quilt has less time-consuming piecing than the other quilts in this book; it is more of a quilting stitch challenge.

Our quilt has a gentle look in soft, subtle shades and is an ideal size for a comforter on the back of a couch, ready to be wrapped around in autumn before you have lit the home fires, or even on cool summer evenings.

MATERIALS REQUIRED:

Cotton material for our embroidered centres and middle square—30 cm (12 in)
3 plain-coloured cottons—30 cm (8 in) of each
Fabric for wide border material—150 cm (60 in) square
Batting—150 cm (60 in)
DMC Stranded cotton—we used 223 on our plum-coloured fabric
Quilting cotton
Plastic for making a template
Stanley knife

Quilt measures 1.44 m (approx. 4½ ft) square

THE EMBROIDERED CENTRES

The Poppy Rose Footstool (instructions on page 66)

On the wrong side of your chosen cotton material draw the sewing line of 14 cm (5½ in) square. Draw a line 5 mm (¼ in) outside this as the cutting line. You will need to make four squares. The material is embroidered before it is cut out.

Enlarge Fig. F on a photocopier by 82%. Trace the pattern on using a soft pencil. For our plum-coloured cotton we worked the stitches in six strands of DMC Stranded cotton—223. Use a colour which matches perfectly the material you have chosen.

The corner stitching is Split Back stitch, as is the outline of the flower motif. The inside of the flower is Lattice Couching. Repeat this stitching for all four centres and cut them out along the cutting line.

CUTTING-OUT PLAN FOR THE TESSELLATED BLOCKS

Trace the template shapes B, C, D, E and F onto stiff plastic, as instructed in the Poultry Quilt. After choosing your three plain colours, trace the templates on the wrong side giving yourself an accurate sewing line. Draw the cutting line 5 mm (¼ in) out from the sewing line.

You will need:
32 pieces of template B
16 pieces of template C
16 pieces of template D (same shape as C but different colour)
16 pieces of template E
36 pieces of template F

The centre square K is a one-off piece, 10 cm square.

SEWING THE TESSELLATED BLOCKS

This is the suggested order for sewing the pieces together:
  i) Join Bs to Cs
 ii) Join 32 Fs to Ds and the 4 remaining Fs to K
iii) Join those joined in (ii) to the embroidered centres
 iv) Join Es into the corners of those formed in (iii)
  v) Add those joined in (i) to those joined in (iv)

JOINING BLOCKS AND BORDERS

It was important with our patterned fabric that the pattern all went the same way. If this is important for your fabric, cut out the following strips of fabric in this order with the pattern running the same way. Remember to draw the sewing and cutting lines on the wrong side of the fabric, with the cutting line 5 mm (¼ in) away from the sewing line.

Opposite: The Carlton Quilt in the barn (instructions start on page 69)

1) 140 cm x 25 cm (56 in x 10 in)
2) 140 cm x 25 cm (56 in x 10 in)
3) 94 cm x 25 cm (37½ in x 10 in)
4) 94 cm x 25 cm (37½ in x 10 in)
5)-8) 40 cm x 14 cm (16 in x 5½ in) x 4 times, but be careful with the pattern

One of the embroidered centres from the Carlton Quilt (instructions start on page 69)

Fig. F Stitches for the embroidered centres. Measures 14 cm square.

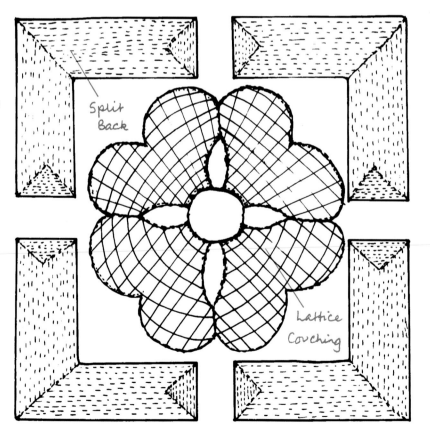

The tessellated tiles on the Carlton Quilt (instructions start on page 69)

THE BLUE BRIAR BRICK

MATERIALS REQUIRED:

A brick (or wooden block of the same dimensions)
Wool wadding to cover brick
Blue fabric—at least 33 cm x 46 cm (13¼ in x 18½ in)
Felt—21 cm x 10 cm (8½ in x 4 in)
DMC Stranded cotton—white, 794 and 791
DMC Perle 5—white, 794 and 791
DMC Broder—white

Trace the pattern onto the blue fabric using a light box.

Start sewing with the briar flower in the centre. Outline each petal in Chain stitch using white DMC Broder. White DMC Perle 5 is then Satin stitched over the top of the Chain stitch. With the Satin stitch over the Chain stitch it is easier to keep the Satin stitch on a line and it makes a puffier look and gives a textured effect. In the centre of the rose, Satin stitch around the circle, and then outline the Satin stitch with a row of Split Back stitch. Surrounding the centre of the flower, sew a row of Cretan stitch to form the stamens using three strands of DMC Stranded cotton in pale blue. On top of the Cretan stitch sew a row of Chain stitch using two strands of DMC Stranded cotton in dark blue, making sure the long part of the Chain stitch lies between the Cretan stitch stamens. Two rows of French Knots are sewn around the edge of the Cretan stitch using white DMC Broder giving the effect of pollen. The third row of pollen is little Seed stitches also in white DMC Broder.

The other briar flower is worked in exactly the same way with the same threads.

All the stems joining the hips and briars are worked in Herringbone stitch using white DMC Broder. The hips are worked in Roumanian Couching in white DMC Broder. The end calyces are worked in Satin stitch in white DMC Broder. The thorns on the stems are straight stitches along the edge.

The smooth-sided leaves are worked in white DMC Perle 5 in Roumanian Couching. The veins are worked in Twisted Chain stitch using dark blue DMC Perle 5.

The serrated-edged leaves are worked with Fly stitch down the middle in pale blue DMC Perle 5. The outside edge of these leaves is white DMC Perle 5 in Buttonhole stitch.

Cover the brick with quilting batting, slip stitched in place and then cover it with your embroidered fabric, sewing down corners and lacing across the bottom. To finish, glue a piece of felt olong the bottom and slip stitch around the edge.

Herringbone

Roumanian
Couching

Satin

Chain covered
by Satin

Cretan

Satin
Split Back

Chain

Twisted Chain

Seed

Buttonhole

Fly

French knots

Roumanian
Couching

CHAPTER ✦ FOUR

THINGS FAMILIAR TO US

It is said that familiarity breeds contempt, but I think we should always be receptive to seeing the ordinary and commonplace afresh and with a new shine on it. With this in mind it was a challenge to work with bush flowers as familiar to us as wattle and eucalyptus and to try to bring out their natural glow. As Emily Dickinson writes

> The Pedigree of Honey
> Does not concern the Bee—
> A clover, any time, to him
> Is aristocracy—

and so it should be with our bright wattle and more subtle eucalyptus. We need no encouragement to enjoy the beauty of these flowers as we roam in the bush of the Tasmanian highlands, the Monaro, the slopes around Corryong or even the hills of home.

One of the reasons we spend time in these particular areas is because our husbands love fly fishing. While not as fanatical about fishing as our spouses, all three of us marvel at the delicacy of the dry and wet fishing flies. We could not resist stitching two from Australia—the Sunset Fly, a wet fly developed by Dr Robert Sloane for particular use in the Tasmanian highlands, and a dry fly, the Dr Wark, a North Eastern Victorian fly developed by the late Sir Ian Wark. The Sunset Fly has heavy yellow tying silk, the tail of a dark possum, and yellow, orange and black dyed hen hackle. The important thing to keep in mind when tying or sewing this fly is that 'the detailed appearance of the fly seems to be unimportant'. The Dr Wark is a hybrid between a beetle and a stonefly and is a favourite of those who fish the beautiful streams of the Merrijig area.

We can also imagine wondrous adaptations of many other flies. Maybe the Ruby Eyed Lacewing, the Orange Stinger,

The Blue Briar Brick (instructions on page 76)

Murrumbidgee Mayfly or the New England Assassin. Once you have mastered the Sunset Fly and Dr Wark you could try any insect or other fishing flies. Work with a magnifying glass and translate the visual into a stitching reality.

Partly in answer to the recession in the wool industry and partly because she is always on the move innovating, Debo decided to market her own wool directly to home knitters. This led to her experimenting with colours and resulted in her beautiful Avago Wool Company selection of wools which you see in various photographs throughout this book. The baby blanket on page 92, Budgerigars for Babies, was sewn using these beautiful wools.

THE GUMNUT FOOTSTOOL
(NOT FOR GUMBOOTS)

We are confronted with eucalyptus wherever we turn in Australia. To us it is emblematic of Australia and prods a twinge of nostalgia in any Australian travelling in the Mediterranean and Californian areas. Though the sewer is frequently shown patterns for embroidering gum blossoms and nuts, we think ours, with its circular shape and its strong leafy structure, is sufficiently different to appeal.

Only four stitches are used—Split Back stitch, Long stitch, French Knots and Stem stitch. In using the particular threads we have chosen, the eucalyptus has been given a delicate touch. This pattern could be used for projects other than a footstool.

MATERIALS REQUIRED:

Thick twill fabric—50 cm (20 in) square
DMC Variegated Stranded cotton—125
DMC Stranded cotton—422, 743, 741, 900, 720, 309, 961, 963, 902 and 816

Enlarge the drawing on page 84 on a photocopier by 121%. Trace the pattern onto a piece of thick, twill-weave, neutral-coloured cotton using a light box.

Leaves

a) On the inside of each leaf sew six threads of DMC Variegated Stranded cotton—125 in Split Back stitch. Be careful not to pull too tight. The middle of the leaf is a row of Split Back stitch sewn in DMC Stranded cotton—422.
b) The outside is Split Back stitch in six threads of 961.

Gum Blossoms

All gum blossoms are sewn using the same long straight stitches. The stitches should vary between 5 mm and 1 cm (¼ in and ½ in). You should place the colours where you prefer, working from the inside out. All stitches in the flowers are six threads of DMC Stranded cotton. Colour numbers are 743, 741, 900, 720, 309, 961, 963, 902 and 816.

c) The centres are worked in straight Long stitch in varying colours. In the very middle are French Knots.
d) Stitch three or four rows of light pink or yellow French Knots around the perimeter of the flower, out from the Long stitches. Stitch darker French Knots over the ends of the Long stitches.

Detail of the embroidery on the Gumnut Footstool (instructions start on page 81)

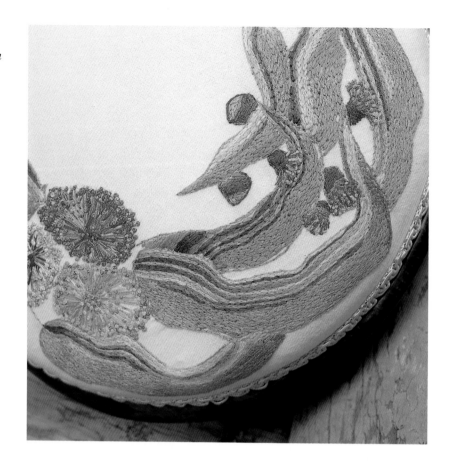

Early working colourwash of the Gumnut Footstool design

Opposite: The Gumnut Footstool

The Wattle Box amongst the wattle

The decorated blue rectangle is finished by edging with yellow piping and then sewn onto a check fabric or one of your choice. The piping is edged with Couching in black DMC Stranded cotton.

The box is constructed as for the Wild Rose Box except the embroidered piece is sewn onto the box lid covering material which is cut 38 cm x 32 cm (15¼ in x 12¾ in), finished size 28 cm x 23 cm (11¼ in x 9¼ in).

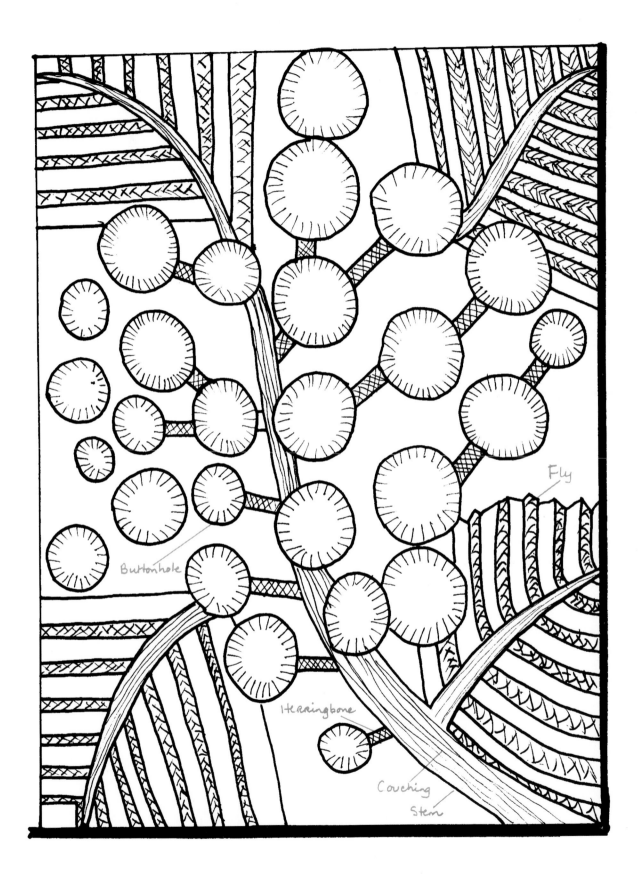

THE DR WARK SHOE BAG

These Australian fishing flies require a bit of creative lateral thinking and sewing. We began by treating them lightly and now we are dead serious about them!

The Dr Wark fly Gail stitched on to a shoe bag made of blue Oxford cloth. In the stitching we misspelt Dr Wark; we had only heard the name of the fly, not seen it in writing! The same shoe bag could have other designs from this book and become something even more glamorous. The colours of the fly were copied using a magnifying glass.

MATERIALS REQUIRED:

Shirting cotton—25 cm (10 in)
Balger thread—005
DMC Stranded cotton—946, 349, 420, 3790, 991, 817 and
    black
DMC Perle 3—420 and Ecru
Rachelette—A19

Enlarge the drawing below on a photocopier by 121%. Trace the outline of the fly drawing onto the cotton. The eye and the shank of the hook are worked in Buttonhole stitch sewn very closely together with one thread of black DMC Stranded cotton or, as used, Balger thread—005 which gives a glowing effect. The red at the head of the body is Satin stitch using 817. The wings are lines of Couching in DMC Perle 3—Ecru, as is the tail. The body is sewn in Satin stitch; we used DMC Stranded cotton—991, with Rachelette—A19 sewn over the top for this particular fly. The hackles are worked at random and where the stitch is too long, catch it down at several intervals with the same thread, which is one thread of any of the DMC Stranded cottons. Overwork the stitches lightly.

Opposite: Shoe and reel bags inspired by fishing flies

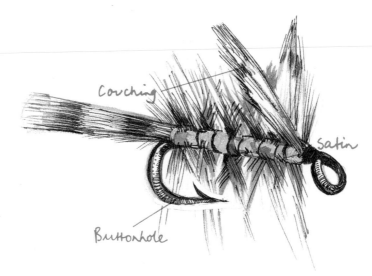

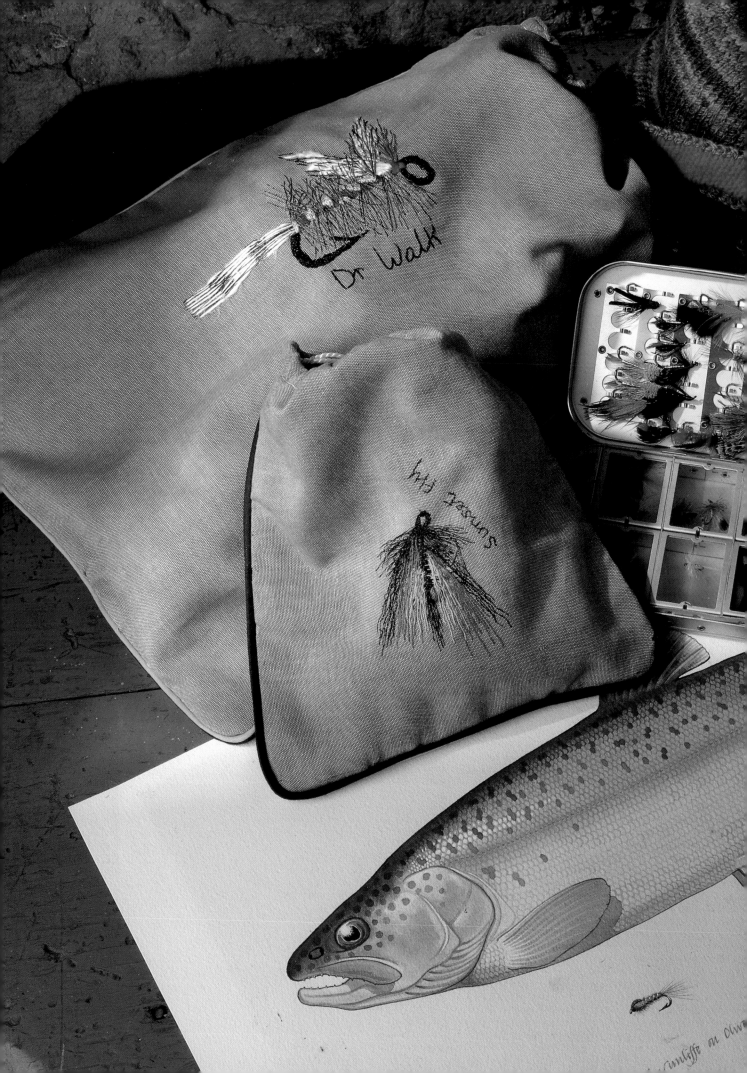

Dr Walk

Sunray fly

THE SUNSET FLY REEL BAG

MATERIALS REQUIRED:

Oxford cloth fabric—25 cm (10 in)
DMC Stranded cotton—946, 444 and 3790
Balger thread—005

The Sunset Fly, exotic as it is, looks great on the cast-off blue Oxford shirting and makes a stylish fly reel bag, though this shape could be ideal for many precious items. You could even pad the material and quilt it for added protection. Look closely at some of the salt-water flies which are usually larger and even more colourful. The Sunset Fly is traced on and sewn using a similar technique to that of the Dr Wark; but first enlarge the illustration on a photocopier by 121%. It is a more vivid fly, so use strong yellows and reds.

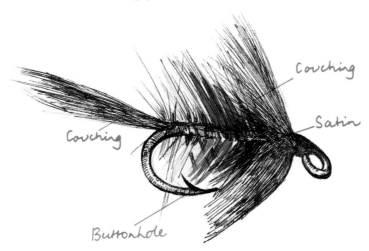

BUDGERIGARS FOR BABIES

This blanket (photograph overleaf) should brighten any baby's day with its vivid budgies instead of the usual pale lambs, bunnies or pastel hearts 'n' roses. Each bird is sewn the same way, using the different hues to gain different effects. Gail worked these birds with a one ply strand unravelled from the thicker ply of Debo's wool. Any variegated, brightly coloured wool will produce the desired effect.

MATERIALS REQUIRED:

1 ply wool in various colours
Watercolours thread—Midnight, Bark
A woollen blanket
A large, blunt-ended tapestry needle

Enlarge drawing below on a photocopier by 270%. Trace the outline of the birds onto the blanket with a soft pencil using a light box. The body of each bird is stitched in Roumanian Couching. The change in direction of the stitches helps create the effect of the body outline, crest, wings and tail feathers. Over the top of some of the feathers, sew Fly stitch and Continuous Fly stitch in different size stitches using Watercolours thread—Midnight to define individual markings. The eyes are outlined in Split Back stitch and the feet are sewn in Roumanian Couching using Watercolours—Bark.

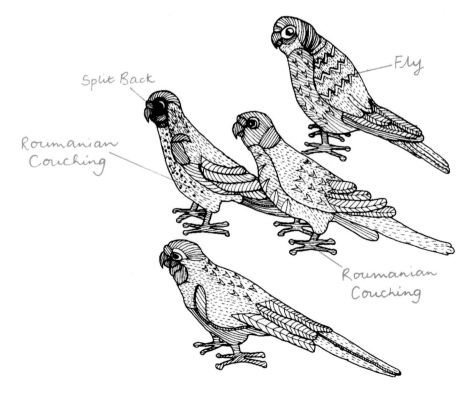

Budgerigar baby blanket (instructions on page 91)

The hues of Debo's hand-dyed wools in the barn

THE DOWAGER'S NEEDLEBOOK

The dowager's needlebook (above) belonged to Debo's English mother-in-law. A descendant of Quaker stock, this wise lady was an eternal optimist. It was 25 years ago that she decided to give her daughter-in-law this beautiful present. Debo could not imagine a more delightful or generous gift. She fingered it delicately and politely offered to 'put it away as a treasure', but her mother-in-law replied, 'You must use it to truly enjoy it'. Her hope was that it would be put to great use as well as be appreciated for its beauty. She was surely optimistic that Debo would be a needleworker one day.

The needlebook is made of pure silk satin and the intricate pattern is sewn in silk threads. It is edged with gold brocade and highlighted with minuscule black sequins. It is made in great style, of materials not of our century. Holding the needlebook is like having a museum in your hand. The pattern is Jacobean...the strong design translates beautifully in patterns for today's embroiderers. The leaves of the book are fine woollen flannel. Some of the original needles were still in the book, with eyes much finer than we would use today.

Accompanying this needlebook was a crochet strawberry 4 cm long, filled with emery. This was used to push your needles into to take the rust spots off, in the days before stainless steel.

Debo has had great pleasure handling this needlebook, using it and never simply being the custodian of it. She is sure her mother-in-law would delight in the thought of the book being the source of inspiration for delicate designs, for she was a lady who enjoyed needlework. Most of all she would enjoy the thought of the design being sewn on useful objects—cushions and throwovers.

THE RED CUSHION AND YELLOW CUSHION

The suggested stitches for both cushions are the same. The design tends to change characteristics with the use of different threads. You can choose your own colours to suit your backing material.

THREADS FOR THE RED CUSHION:

DMC Perle 5—817, 917, 3051, 986, 725 and 327
DMC Stranded Cotton—830, 327, 817, 550, 603, 816 and
    black
Watercolours threads—Tobacco, Meadow and Flame
Rochelle—Gold
Rachelette—Crimson

The stitches for the Red Cushion are sewn onto a panel of fabric of your choice (enlarge the patterns on a photocopier by 122% and trace onto your material). This panel is then sewn onto the cushion fabric. If you choose to finish the cushion with Italian quilting the instructions are in the Stitch Glossary.

THREADS FOR THE YELLOW CUSHION:

DMC Stranded cotton—720, 900 and 928
DMC Perle 5—503 and 3072
Jenny Thompson—470 and 725
DMC Soft cottons—2233, 2734, 2759, 2309, 2926, 2829,
    2727, 2745, 2839, 2767, 2730, 2726, 2325, 2833 & Ecru

These stitches are sewn directly onto your cushion material. Enlarge the patterns on page 98 on a photocopier by 141% and trace onto your material.

THE FLOWERS

Zinnia

The outside petals are Satin stitch. The inside petals are outlined in Buttonhole stitch. The centre of the flower is Stem stitched.

Celandine

The petals are individually worked in Herringbone stitch. The base of the flower is French Knots. On the Yellow Cushion a row of black chain stitch is sewn between the base and petals.

The Red Cushion

The embroidered panel on the Italian-quilted Red Cushion (embroidery instructions start on page 94, quilting instructions appear in the Stitch Glossary)

The embroidered Yellow Cushion (instructions start on page 94)

Opposite: The Red Cushion in the barn

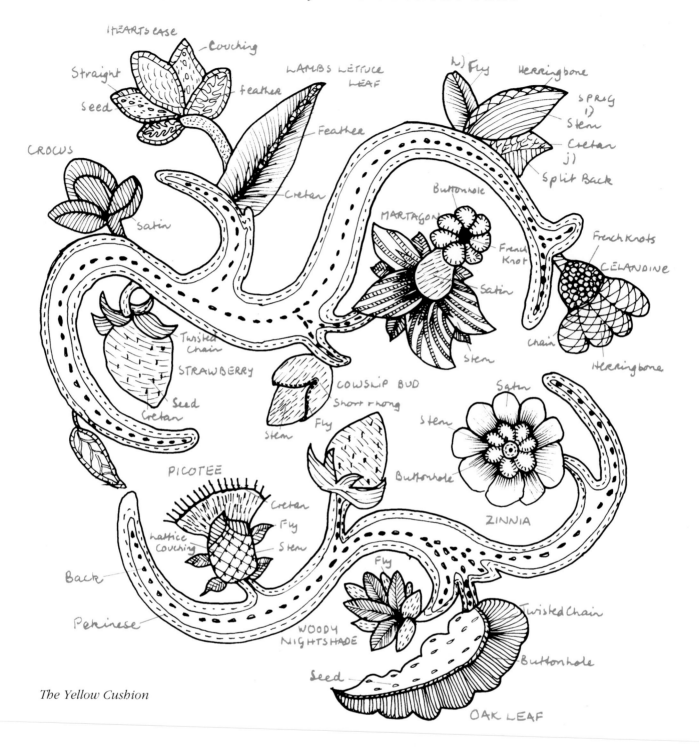

The Yellow Cushion

Woody Nightshade

The seven petals are Fly stitched. On the Yellow Cushion, the divided base is Fly stitch too. On the Red Cushion the base is worked around in Stem stitch. The top half is filled in with Lattice Couching. The bottom half has seven Long stitches worked in to the centre.

Heartsease

The petals are outlined in Couching. The three large petals are filled with Feather stitch. The two smaller petals have little straight stitches down the centre and on the Yellow Cushion some Seed stitches as well.

Lamb's Lettuce Leaves

a) This part is worked in Cretan stitch.
b) This part is rows of Stem stitch.

On the yellow cushion the leaf has a vein of black Feather stitch worked down the middle.

Young Bud

This bud is worked in Fly stitch.

Acanthus Leaf

This leaf is outlined in Twisted Chain stitch with a row of Buttonhole down the centre. One side is filled with Cloud Filling stitch.

Spotted Stem

This stem is worked around in Pekinese stitch with the centre on the red cushion filled in with dispersed French Knots. The centre of the stem on the yellow cushion is spaced Back stitch.

Pimpernel

The five petals are outlined in Stem stitch and filled in with one big Lazy Daisy stitch.

Medlar

This flower is four rows of Short and Long stitch.

Crocus

The petals are Satin stitch and the green calyx on the Red Cushion is rows of Stem stitch.

Strawberry

The calyx of the flower is worked in Twisted Chain stitch. The strawberry is Cretan stitched, with the spots being Seed stitches.

Primrose Leaf

Sew down one side in Buttonhole stitch, and the other side in Split Back stitch.

Martagon

All the petals are worked in rows of Stem stitch. The round centre is Satin stitched. The little top petals are outlined in Buttonhole stitch with a French Knot centre.

Picotee

The base is outlined in Stem stitch with the inside filled in with Lattice Couching. The side wings are worked in Fly stitch. The flower head is worked in three rows of interlacing Cretan stitch.

Pear

This is worked in four rows of Short and Long stitch.

Cowslip Bud

The base is two rows of Short and Long stitch, while the petals are worked in rows of Stem stitch. On the yellow cushion a row of black Fly stitch is sewn between the base and petals.

Oak Leaf

One half is worked in Buttonhole stitch. The other half is outlined in Twisted Chain stitch, with a row of this stitch also down the middle. This half is filled with Seed stitches.

Branch of Leaves

This is sewn with a combination of stitches:
 c) Outline in Stem stitch
 d) Cretan stitch
 e) Rows of Stem stitch
 f) Outline in Stem stitch and fill with Cloud Filling stitch
 g) Satin stitch

Sprig

 h) Fly stitch
 i) Half the leaf is sewn in Herringbone stitch, while the other half is Stem stitch
 j) A row of Cretan stitch outlined down one side in Split Back stitch

Pear Leaf

Red Cushion:
 k) This part of the leaf is outlined in Twisted Chain stitch filled in with a row of Feather stitch
 l) One row of Fly stitch

The pear leaf on the Yellow Cushion is outlined in Twisted Chain stitch filled in with a row of Feather stitch.

Embroidered Border on Red Cushion

Each section is outlined in Couching, next to a row of Back stitch with regular spacings. Then another two rows of Couching completes the border.

FINISHING THE CUSHIONS

Once the stitching is complete, the cushions are ready to be made up. The red cushion can have Italian quilting (see Stitch Glossary), as ours did, and piping or cording around the outside. We added braid to our yellow cushion.

THE DOWAGER'S WRAP

Having sewn the Needlebook pattern on two quite distinct cushions we decided to show how the design takes on a different look when sewn on wool, in wools. We had great difficulty in deciding whether this piece should be called a throw, a knee rug or a comforter, but we finally decided on 'wrap'. The particular piece of wool we chose also proved tricky. It is a lovely khaki colour, however, when Gail sewed light blues on it the yellow of the background became prominent. Other chosen colours changed the 'non colour' background into a colour not to our liking. As you sew you learn a lot about colour. The inspirations for the final selection of colours came from an old Flemish painting which had exactly the same colour background as the wool flannel.

MATERIALS REQUIRED:

Fine wool flannel—150 cm x 145 cm (60 in x 58 in)
Appletons wools—yellows—692, 695 and 693; greens—
    331, 241, 245 and 243; blues—321, 325 and 328;
    pinks—223, 224, 226 and 221; red—865
Needle—Bohin—Chenille Avec Pointe

Lightly mark a 13 cm (5¼ in) square onto the centre of your flannel. Enlarge the four illustrations on a photocopier by 148%. Trace the pattern around the square with a 5B pencil using a light box as shown in Fig. G.

The pears are sewn first in Roumanian Couching, starting with a row of 695; a row of 693 is worked into this first row to give a shaded effect. A row of 692 is then worked back into the 693. To form the bottom tip of the pear sew five Long stitches working out from the centre in 695, then a couple of green Long stitches in 243 also working out from the centre. A row of Long stitches is worked around the hip of the pear in 223 and 865. The first leaf of the pear is Chain stitch in 245. One half of the second leaf is in 245 and the other half is sewn in 243 in Chain stitch also. A row of Fly stitch is sewn down the centre of both leaves in 241.

The leaf opposite the pear is worked in interlaced Cretan stitch using the three lighter greens. The three greens are gradually worked into each other with the Cretan stitch to give a shaded effect. The veins are sewn in 245 in Twisted Chain stitch. The stem joining the leaf to the S-bend is sewn in Herringbone stitch in 243.

1. The Pears

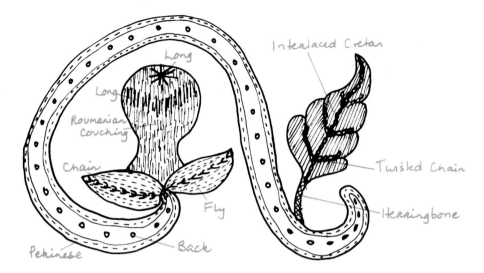

The pink flowers are worked next. The petals are Short and Long stitch using the three pinks. The green bud of the flower is sewn in Roumanian Couching in 241, and the stem in small Satin stitch in the same wool. A row of Buttonhole stitch is worked at the base of the petal, working into the green bud in 226. This same colour is Stem stitched around the petals to outline them. Colours 226 and 865 are Couched in loops at the bottom of the petals—you can see this on the drawing.

The leaves on the other side of the S-bend are worked next. The leaf nearest the flower is in Buttonhole stitch on one side in 243, while the other side is outlined in Split Back stitch in 245, with Seed stitch filling it in. The outside leaf is worked in three rows of Chain stitch in 243 then three rows of Chain stitch in 245 and a row of Buttonhole stitch in 243.

The sides of the bell-shaped blue flowers are outlined in Split Back stitch in 328 and 325. At the waist, small Herringbone stitches are worked in 321. The distinct points in the flower are sewn in Satin stitch in 321. Above the points a row of Cretan stitch is sewn in 325. In between the points and the Cretan stitches, Seed stitches are sewn. The stamens are

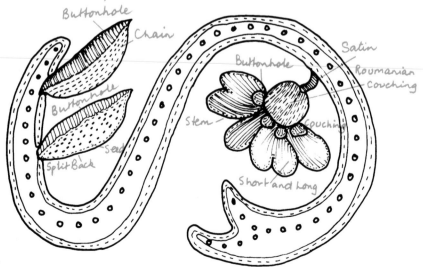

2. The Pink Flowers

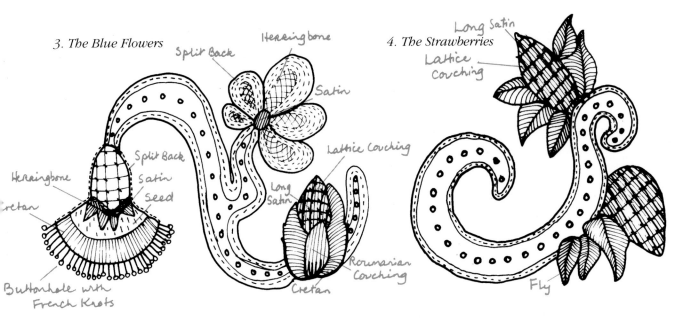

3. The Blue Flowers

4. The Strawberries

Buttonhole stitch in 328 with a row of French Knots out from the end in 321.

The clover leaves opposite the blue flowers are five separate segments. Each segment is outlined in two rows of Split Back stitch in 241 and one row of the same stitch and colour across the tip of the segment. Sew two rows of Split Back stitch inside these three rows using 243. The middle gap in each segment is filled with Herringbone stitch using 245. Where the segments meet is a round circle sewn in Satin stitch in 245. The bud at the

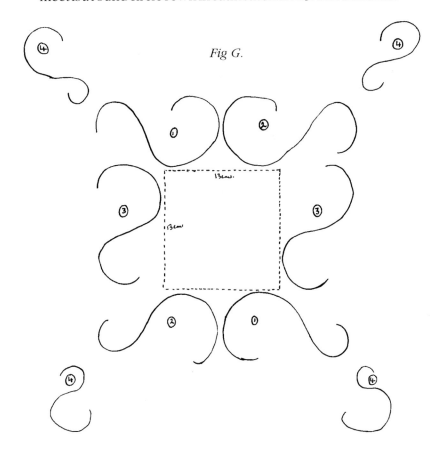

Fig G.

The woollen Dowager's Wrap (instructions start on page 101)

end of this curve has three leaves encasing the bud. The two outside leaves are sewn in Cretan stitch in 243. The inside lighter green leaf is worked in Roumanian Couching in 241. The outline of the leaves and bud is Stem stitch in 328. The bud is sewn in long Satin stitch in 331 with Lattice Couching in 221 over the top. The Couching is caught down with 865. You will find the Couching holds the long Satin stitches in place.

The S-bends are worked next in Pekinese stitch using 695 for the Back stitch and 693 for the Interlacing. The dots inside the S-bends are spaced Back stitches in two threads of 328 worked together.

The strawberries are worked next in long Satin stitch sewn the length of the berry in 865. Lattice Couching is sewn over to hold the Satin stitches down using 223 caught down with 695. All the leaves of the strawberries are Fly stitch in the three shades of 245, 243 and 241, with each leaf a different green. The S-bend with the strawberries is worked the same as the other S-bends.

The flannel is lined with fine lawn or silk. You can either put braid around the edge, or Buttonhole stitch around the edge, or you could bring your lining from the back 1 cm (½ in) over to the front and Slip stitch it as invisibly as possible.

CHAPTER ✺ SIX

AMONGST FRIENDS

A few years ago a group of us who spend January together and meet to stitch each week, decided to make a quilt epitomising the seaside town where we summered. With great trepidation we each chose our own view and wondered how we could transform it into reality. That was the humble start for many of us.

The Retreat
South Quilt

THE BARWON HEADS QUILT

The beach rotunda, marrum grass on the bluff, river pelicans and windsurfers, the windswept surf beach, colourful caravaners, the Ozone jetty, the golf course clubhouse and the Fisherman's Co-operative were sketched on 25 cm (10 in) squares of tracing paper. It was decided that a uniform fabric for the sky would link the blocks in the quilt, and we could not resist the texture and colour of cast-off school shirts—an Oxford blue cloth, which was perfect for summer skies.

Gail helped each of us to plan our appliqué picture, arranging colours and showing us how to needleturn under the simple designs. Some of us studied incompetence in those days. Gail was kept busy with SOS calls over tea-tree fences and through open front doors.

When we met with our squares in metamorphosis, a buzz of chatter, the odd squeal of laughter and most importantly, an exchange of ideas took place. This is the beauty of group projects—suggestions are generated and beginners are given confidence by encouragement. Each square was completed with an individual stamp on it. It was then a matter of joining the squares with stripping material and attaching a border. We had created a quilt top. We added batting and a cotton backing and jointly quilted it.

Looking back on this wall quilt (see photograph on page 109), after a few years of sewing, we can see what raw beginners we were. The quilt's appeal is its coastal, naive quality. A 'story' grows around the quilt and one day it may even become 'historic'. The Fisherman's Co-operative may be pulled down for a fancy fish restaurant, the living room which looks out on the pelicans gliding on the river has burnt down and the jetty has since been taken down and rebuilt. Our quilt is a recording of a moment in time, as well as being a reminder that natural things fortunately change very little.

THE RETREAT SOUTH QUILT

The next year—1990—Gail left us in summer to camp up at Corryong. We all wondered what we would do without her. It was suggested we quietly make her a quilt as a form of thanks for all she had taught us. We would show her we could do it on our own. We decided a 'Retreat South' quilt (see photograph on page 105) was in order, this being the name of the Bett property.

Our group knew Retreat South well and photographs were secretly taken of buildings and views from various angles. To these images we added our poetic licence. Again, we decided to unify the quilt with Oxford blue skies and to use a bright red Les Olivades fabric for the stripping. At the top is the 'white' garden into which the stitcher, rather a colourful character, insisted on putting colour. Because the splendid embroidery on this square was thickly encrusted it seemed best to place the bare Barrabool Hills next to it. On the next row down is the RS branded cow and a looming cactus which Gail was showing partiality toward, the homestead with Jenny the sheepdog, and on the right the Hampshire Down sheep are represented. The next row has Max's pumpkin patch, the potting shed and vegetable garden, a layer on the nest, and the view looking down to the water through the rose garden. On the bottom row is a goat in front of the barn where we sew upstairs. Next to this is one square we all chuckle about warmly. It is Gail quilting in her yellow room; a square appliquéd by her mother Joyce. The Fantail pigeons and dovecote, and the pig in the corner, complete the scenes. The Ohio stars in the top corners were chosen to balance the quilt and because this was a popular work amongst our quilting group. The Ohio star block was also a symbol of adventuring, and that is exactly what we were doing!

It was a considerable challenge keeping this project a secret from Gail once she was back from Corryong, as she is the nucleus of all our sewing activities and is a great sniffer of secrets! The quilt was stripped and quilted over a few months by three of us and given to Gail for her birthday. It was never meant to be a quilt for her house, but we hoped it would be perfect for the stone barn wall where it hangs today.

*The Barwon Heads Quilt—a recording
of a moment in time*

STITCH GLOSSARY

APPLIQUÉ

There are many ways to appliqué by hand. Gail prefers the method used by the makers of the old Baltimore quilts. Use fine quality cotton, which has been washed and ironed, for your patches. Use fine thread in a colour which matches the appliqué patch, rather than the background material.

First, draw your shape on the right side of the fabric as per the instructions in each project. Cut out 5 mm (¼ in) all the way around and snip this patch with very sharp scissors up to the drawing line, especially on the curves. Where there is a sharp point, cut the fabric away diagonally across the point so there will be as little bulk as possible under the point.

Pin the appliqué patches where they are to go on the design. Thread a needle with thread which matches the patch. Starting at a straight edge or a gently rounded edge, Slip stitch it, turning the edge under with the tip of the needle as you sew. As you do this hold the edge down with your left thumb nail— having a reasonably long nail helps! The drawn line should be barely out of sight.

To sew the stitch, bring the needle up through the two layers of fabric and then insert it right next to where it came up. Run the thread under the back of the fabric and up for the next stitch, 2.5 mm (⅛ in) away. In this way the long stitch is hidden at the back of your work. Pull the thread firmly, but not so severely as to pucker the patches.

Where sharp points occur, stitch right to the point, turn the fabric around and stitch the other side of the point, 'needle turning' the fabric under.

BACK STITCH

This stitch is used for lines and outlines. All the stitches should be of equal length and firmly sewn. The stitch is worked from right to left. Bring the needle up at 1, insert the needle at 2, then up at 3, thus taking a step back, and so on. Make sure the stitch goes back into the hole made by the previous stitch.

BULLION KNOT

This knot serves a similar purpose to the French Knot although it is larger and heavier and gives an embossed look. Bullion Knots require quite a bit of practice to perfect them. It might be best to try them first with a thickish thread and a thick needle with a narrow eye, such as a Chenille needle.

Bring the needle up at 1 and insert it at 2 at the length you want the bullion coil, then bring it up exactly at 1 again. Do not put the needle right through, let it lie on its side and twist the thread round and round clockwise. Seven or eight twists are about right, although it depends on the length of the initial stitch. Place your left thumb and index finger on the twists and carefully pull the needle and thread through the twists until all the loose thread is taken up. Next, pull the needle and thread away in opposite directions and let go. Tighten it up and then pass the needle through to the back at 2.

BUTTONHOLE STITCH

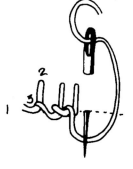

Bring the needle up at 1, then insert it at 2, then up at 3, making sure the thread is under the needle before you pull it through. Repeat in this way. Be careful not to bunch up too much fabric between 2 and 3 or the stitch does not have the right effect. Work this stitch from left to right. The looped edge makes this stitch successful for edging to prevent fraying, for example, in appliqué.

CHAIN STITCH

Chain stitch can be used as an outline stitch or as a filling when used in close rows.

Bring the needle up at 1, insert it very close to 1. Holding the thread to the left with your left thumb, bring the needle up at 2. As you pull the thread to make the stitch make sure the thread is under the needle as in the drawing.

Work this stitch towards yourself. Make sure the needle is always inserted into the same hole as that through which the thread emerges. The stitches should be of equal length.

CLOUD FILLING STITCH

As the name suggests, this is a filling stitch and is made up of small stitches placed at regular intervals—into these stitches a thread is laced by taking it under an upper stitch and then under a lower stitch. Alternate rows are laced so that the loops meet under the same stitch. This is made clearer if you look at the drawing. The look of this stitch may vary a lot due to the

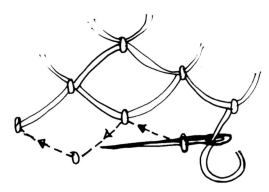

spacing of the foundation stitches—a closely woven effect can be created or an airy, open impression.

COUCHING

This is an interesting stitch for lines, outlines or borders.

For the base thread or threads, bring the needle up at 1 and allow the thread to lie upon the fabric. Hold this thread with your left thumb while working the line to prevent looping or puckering. For the tying thread, bring the needle up at 2 and right next to here insert at 3 so there is only a thread difference between 2 and 3. Next, bring the needle up at 4, down at 5 and so on, as in the drawing. These stitches should be taut.

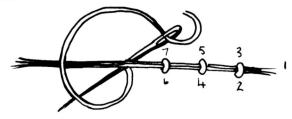

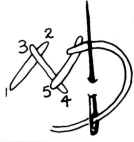

CRETAN STITCH

Cretan stitch is economical of thread and is wonderful for filling shapes when worked close together. The needle comes up at 1. With the thread on your right-hand side insert the needle at 2 and up at 3, down at 4 and up at 5 and so on. Work this stitch from left to right.

CROSS-HATCHING

Faintly draw crossing lines an equal width apart across the material you are working on and stitch with a tiny running or quilting stitch. The width apart will vary with each project.

DAISY OR DETACHED CHAIN STITCH

Bring the needle up at 1, hold the thread to the left with the left thumb, insert the needle close to 1, bring needle through at 2 and as you pull the thread to make the stitch the thread should be under the needle. Make a small stitch to hold the loop by inserting the needle at 3.

When the Detached Chain stitches are sewn in a circular pattern the stitch is called a Lazy Daisy Stitch.

FEATHER STITCH

Bring the needle up at 1 and insert at 2 holding the thread to the left with your left thumb. Bring the needle up at 3 making sure you go over the thread as in the drawing. It makes a neater look if 2 is opposite 1 where the thread has come through the fabric. Work this movement from left to right alternately. Work the stitch towards yourself.

FLY STITCH

Bring the needle up at 1, insert it at 2, holding the thread with your left thumb bring the needle up at 3. As you pull the thread to make the stitch take care that the thread is under the needle as in drawing (a). Insert the needle at 4 as in drawing (b). This

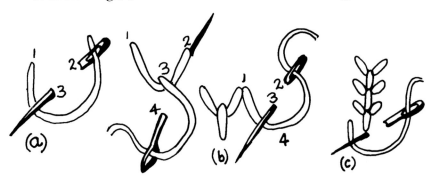

final 'tying' stitch can be different lengths to produce different impressions. Continuous Fly stitch is shown in (c) and is a repetition of the directions just given. This continuous Fly stitch can be 'closed' or worked close together for a heavy, dense effect. An Open Fly stitch is one where the stitches are spaced well apart, giving a lighter, lacy effect.

FRENCH KNOT

French Knots are useful for filling areas where a texture is required and they are excellent anywhere that the effect of a single dot is needed, for example in a bird's eye. The French Knot requires practice—the twist of the needle and a taut thread are important elements in successful French Knots. Bring the needle up at 1, twist the thread around the needle and insert the needle at 2. Pull the thread which is around the needle gently so it lies flush to the material surface and then pull the needle through to the back of the material.

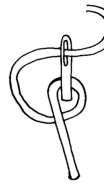

FRENCH KNOT ON A TAIL

This stitch is executed the same way as the French Knot. To form the tail after circling the needle with the thread, insert it to the length you want the tail to be from where the needle first emerged. Pull the thread gently through to the back.

HERRINGBONE STITCH

The needle comes up at 1. Keeping the thread on your right-hand side, insert the needle at 2 and up at 3, down at 4 and up at 5, and so on. Work this stitch from left to right along imagined parallel lines. This is not a difficult stitch, however it is important to keep the stitches an even length apart. This stitch can be worked close together and is then known as Closed Herringbone. When it is spaced apart it is known as Open Herringbone.

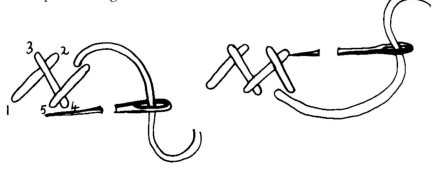

INTERLACED CHAIN STITCH

This stitch is great for a solid border such as we have on the Tartan Curtain Keeper. It is not as difficult as it looks. Make a line of Chain stitches. Anchor the last loop as though you are continuing, but instead of making another loop, insert the needle into the fabric to form an anchoring stitch. See A on the drawings. Now, maybe using a different coloured thread, about four times as long as the chain line, and using a blunt end needle, start the interlacing chain. Bring the needle through the fabric at 1, take it under the second link of the chain and return it under the first link and itself, as shown on the drawing on the left.

Then take the needle under the third link and back under the second link as shown in the drawing on the right. Continue

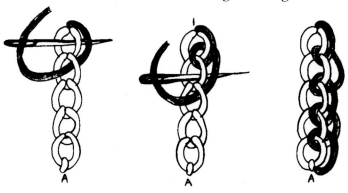

this way without ever inserting the needle into the fabric until you arrive at the end of the chain where you should insert the needle near A on the drawing.

Now repeat this down the left side of the chain.

ITALIAN QUILTING

Two lines 5 mm (¼ in) apart are drawn at intervals of 7 cm (2¾ in) diagonally both ways across the cushion top. The cushion top is then tacked to a piece of cotton backing. With a quilting stitch, sew down each row 5 mm (¼ in) apart and through both thicknesses of material. This stitching forms channels through which a soft cord is then threaded. The cord is drawn through the channels working from the wrong side of the fabric (see the photograph on page 96). Use a large-eyed blunt needle for this task.

LATTICE COUCHING

This is a 'filling' stitch and gives an open effect for the centre of flowers such as those in the Dowager's Needlebook group. Make a lattice effect first with long, evenly spaced stitches sewn horizontally and vertically. At the point where the threads intersect, Couch or sew a small slanting stitch. This last stitch can be effective in a contrasting colour.

LAZY DAISY STITCH

For the instructions for this stitch please look under Daisy or Detached Chain stitch.

PEKINESE STITCH

This stitch, which is also called Chinese stitch, is very suitable for gold or fancy thread as the interlaced thread does not enter the fabric except at the beginning and end of a line and is therefore an economical use of the thread. This stitch can be used as a line stitch or as a solid filler and looks effective as a braid.

The stitch is worked on a foundation line of Back stitches. Into these, another thread is laced as in the drawing. The loops should not be as loose as they appear—they should be pulled firmly.

ROUMANIAN COUCHING ·

This is a 'filling' stitch which is good for large areas, for example in stitching the pheasants' feathers or in areas too long for a Satin stitch.

The needle comes up at 1 and is inserted at 2 in one long stitch. Work your way back along the stitch, up at 3 and insert the needle at 4, close to the original Long stitch. These

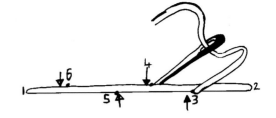

stitches should be angled so they are hardly seen. Fill the shape with row after row worked close together.

SATIN STITCH

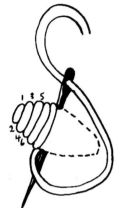

This appears a simple stitch but it is quite difficult to sew correctly and neatly. The stitches are best if they are worked close together and should not be longer than 1.5 cm (¾ in) or they will look bedraggled and will not provide a firm edge to the shape being filled.

Bring the needle up at 1, then insert the needle at 2, up at 3, down at 4 and so on.

When using this stitch for flowers, each petal should be worked in a different direction—this gives light and shade to the work and an effect of relief to the shape.

SEED STITCH

This is a 'filling in' stitch for spaces which have been outlined with another stitch. It is a small, evenly spaced Back stitch, however it can also be sewn at random giving a dotty effect. Make the stitches fairly small and repeat the stitch over the first by using the same stitch holes.

SHORT AND LONG STITCH

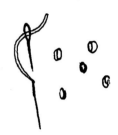

Short and Long stitch is worked similarly to Satin stitch and is so named because of the different stitches which are used for the first row. See 1 on the drawing where a Short and Long stitch is sewn alternately. After finishing the outline of the space to be filled, Satin stitches of equal length are sewn to fill the spaces left by the first row of stitches—see 2. The length of the Satin stitch remains the same except if you are filling odd shapes. The outer line of this stitch forms a regular line and the inner line is irregular. This is useful for a shading effect as different colours can interlock into the first row, resulting in light and dark tonings.

SPLIT BACK STITCH

This is a useful stitch for making narrow lines and outlines and is a good filling stitch, especially where shading is required.

Bring the needle up at 1 and insert it at 2 to form the first stitch. Now bring the needle through this stitch at 3, splitting the strands of the first stitch in the middle. Repeat this along a line.

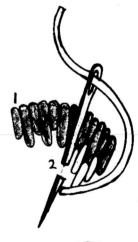

STEM STITCH

An easy stitch which is good for outlining and when used in rows it is a useful 'filling' stitch.

Bring the needle up at 1, then insert it at 2, up at 3 and so on. All the stitches should be the same length and angle. Work this stitch from left to right.

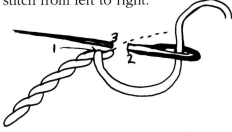

TURKEY WORK STITCH

We use this stitch to give a brushy effect to the centre of the sunflowers. It is worked in rows from left to right. Insert the

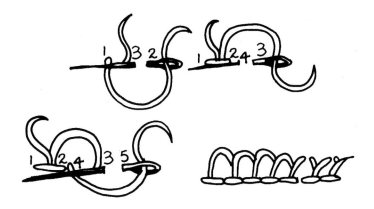

needle at 1, leave 2 cm (1 in) of thread above the fabric and bring the needle up at 2. Insert the needle at 3 with the thread below the needle and bring up at 1 leaving a loop. Make a firm stitch. Insert the needle at 4 and bring out at 3 with the thread above the needle. With the thread below the needle, insert at 5 and continue in this way making rows of loops filling the area required. Snip the top of these loops for the brushy, velvety effect.

TWISTED CHAIN STITCH

This stitch is useful for outlines and borders. Work this stitch downwards or towards yourself. Bring the needle up at 1. Holding the thread with your left thumb, insert the needle at 2, bring it up at 3 and through the loop thus formed. You are now ready for the second stitch.

WHIPPING STITCH

A contrasting coloured thread which is sewn around existing stitching but *not* through the fabric.

BIBLIOGRAPHY

Gans Rueden, E., *Iranian Carpets—Art, Craft and History*. Thames & Hudson, 1978.

Hinson, D.A., *American Graphics—Quilt Design*. Arco Publishing, 1983.

Luce, William, *The Belle of Amherst*. Houghton Mifflin, 1976.

Coysh, Arthur Wilfred, *Blue and White Transfer Printed Earthenware—1780 to 1840*. Newton Abbot, Devon, 1970.

BOOKS GAIL ENJOYS USING:

Nichols, Marion, *Encyclopedia of Embroidery Stitches, Including Crewel*. Dover Publications Inc, 1974.

Beck, Thomasina, *The Embroiderer's Garden*. David & Charles Craft Book, 1988.

Beck, Thomasina, *The Embroiderer's Flowers*. David & Charles Craft Book, 1992.

Ward, L., *Lalla Ward's Countryside Embroidery Book*. Pelham Books, 1989.